# AMBUSH THE ENEMY
## EXPOSING DEMONIC FORCES

## Robin Dinnanauth

© Copyright 2013, Robin Dinnanauth

All Rights Reserved.

No part of this book may be reproduced, stored in a retrieval system, or transmitted by any means, electronic, mechanical, photocopying, recording, or otherwise, without written permission from the author.

ISBN: 978-0-985-36644-5

All scripture quotations, unless otherwise indicated, are taken from the Holy Bible Verses, New King James Version. Copyright © 1982 Thomas Nelson, Inc. Used by permission. All rights reserved.

# Contents

Preface ........................................................................................... v
Introduction ................................................................................ vii
Chapter One: Deliverance from Spiritual Forces ......................... 1
Chapter Two: The Deception in the Spiritual Realm .................. 9
Chapter Three: Spiritual Strategies Against You ....................... 23
Chapter Four: Standing Against Spiritual Forces ...................... 31
Chapter Five: Understanding Deliverance ................................. 55
Chapter Six: The Armor of God ................................................ 61
- Teach Us to Pray
- The Armor of God
- Dress for Battle

Chapter Seven: Your Spiritual Authority .................................. 77
Chapter Eight: Militant and Spiritual Warfare Prayers ............. 83
- Prayer for Forgiveness ..................................................... 83
- Prayer for Deliverance from the Power of Sin ................ 87
- Prayer for Deliverance from Soul Ties ........................... 88
- Prayer for Deliverance from Spiritual Forces ................. 84
- Prayer for Healing from Sickness ................................... 89
- Prayer for Divine and Perfect Health .............................. 91
- Prayer Against Financial Crisis ...................................... 91
- Prayer for Financial Breakthrough .................................. 92
- Prayer for Spiritual House Cleaning ............................... 93

- Prayer for Children ............................................................... 95
- Prayer to Release Godly Spirits ......................................... 98
- Prayer to Be Made Whole from Brokenness ..................... 98

Declaration ....................................................................... 109
About the Author ............................................................. 113
Notes ................................................................................ 115

# Preface

This book "Ambush the Enemy: Exposing Demonic Forces" is a blueprint for combating spiritual forces in your daily life. By thoroughly applying this book's principles to your daily life, you will experience the personal deliverance that Christ died to give you. "And the Lord will deliver me from every evil work and preserve me for His heavenly kingdom. To Him be glory forever and ever. Amen!" (2 Timothy 4:18) Understanding the purpose of deliverance will allow you to break the chains of bondage over your life, liberate you from the toxic influence of spiritual forces, deny the enemy access to you, and catapult you into a victorious life. Jesus was anointed and sent forth to preach deliverance to the captive. "The Spirit of the Lord is upon Me, because He has anointed Me to preach the gospel to the poor; He has sent Me to heal the brokenhearted, to proclaim liberty to the captives and recovery of sight to the blind, to set at liberty those who are oppressed" (Luke 4:18).

In this book, you will discover four elements that play a crucial part in understanding deliverance. Such elements include inner healing, tearing down strongholds, removing legal rights, and commanding demons to go.

Have you been abused, rejected, wounded or hurt in any way? You may be carrying an emotional wound that requires healing. Spiritual forces use such wounds as a breeding ground to attack your weaknesses as well as to imprison and deceive you so that you can grant them permission to reenter your life. In order to restore the brokenness, it is essential that you enter a phase of inner healing.

Once the enemy has deceived you with his trickery, strongholds envelop your life. These strongholds lead you to believe that your dejected situation ought to be a permanent fixture in your life. Strongholds are the residential realm under which demons operate to torment and affect the peace of a person's environment. This book will provide you with a deeper understanding of what is a stronghold and ways in which you can eradicate those that may have emerged in your life. When strongholds are not destroyed, this leads to stagnation in your deliverance and spiritual imprisonment.

Besides strongholds, demons manifest themselves when they are granted legal rights to occupy your life. When undertaking the process of casting out demons, it is essential to address the legal rights at stake. I will provide you with a list of the top legal rights that afflict people today and strategies to *extinguish* them from your life. Just as not following through on destroying your strongholds can impede your deliverance, the same applies for legal rights.

# Introduction

A great spiritual war is being waged against your life. This is a critical invisible battle taking place in the spiritual realm. The Bible states that God's people are destroyed because of lack of knowledge according to Hosea 4:6: "My people are destroyed for lack of knowledge. Because you have rejected knowledge, I also will reject you from being priest for me; because you have forgotten the law of your God, I also will forget your children." Many believers are losing the fight, because they lack knowledge in the area of spiritual warfare and deliverance.

Spirituality was based on warfare during the period of the early Church. The New Testament is filled with military terminology. God's Word was viewed like armor which protected His people from the attacks of Satan. Using faith as the basis to fight the enemy, the early Church engaged in good warfare during its battles.

This spiritual battle has not ended. It is evident in many areas of the church today. We are often focused on getting rich quickly, prosperity, and fighting one another as the battle intensifies around us. With the end of time drawing near, it is of utmost importance that we direct our attention to understanding spiritual warfare. The Apostle Paul warned us in 2 Timothy 3:1: "But know this, that in the last days perilous times will come."

Preparing for these perilous times requires you to learn the strategies of spiritual warfare. Your Christian life is a war. The sooner you recognize and prepare for it, the sooner you will experience victory. Luke 14:31 says, "Or what king, going to make war against another king, does not sit down first and consider whether he is able with ten thousand to meet him who comes against him with twenty thousand?"

No king ever entered into a battle without carefully examining his resources and warfare strategies. In this book, you will discover the strategies, weapons, and power available to you to wage and win the war against your enemy, Satan.

# Chapter One:
# Deliverance from Spiritual Forces

"Whose minds the god of this age has blinded, who do not believe, lest the light of the gospel of the glory of Christ, who is the image of God, should shine on them."

2 Corinthians 4:4

Many people go through their daily lives under spiritual bondage, and they do not know how to liberate themselves. Believing that this captivity is physical rather than spiritual, they seek medical assistance to remedy their spiritual disease. If you are under the influence of demonic forces or are spiritually confined, such a situation cannot be dealt with physically. When faced with an invisible situation in the spiritual realm, it is imperative that you address your case spiritually and seek deliverance.

**What is deliverance?** Deliverance is the act of shutting the doors to the enemy in your life. It destroys every satanic activity in your life and surroundings, reverses every heavy burden you carry, and releases you from spiritual prison. Your spiritual freedom will usher you into a life of total restoration, where personal possessions that were stolen by the enemy will be returned to you. Additionally, all curses and spells that were cast upon your life will be broken and sent back to their original sources. Thus, allowing you to move from failure into total victory in every aspect of your life.

**Who needs deliverance?** Are you sick and the doctors are unable to identify what's wrong with you? If your answer is "yes," this means you are suffering from a spiritual sickness. Did your mother have a difficult pregnancy with you? Were you conceived during a relationship of adultery or fornication? Did you endure a childhood of abuse? Were you raped or molested? Did you almost die during your early childhood? Did you have imaginary friends when you were a child? Have you ever participated in abortion procedures? Did you or your parents experience poverty at any point in life? Have you seen a specific trend of problems occurring in your family? Are you obsessed with visiting palm readers, satanic advisors, and psychics? Do you experience chronic headaches or bouts of confusion? Are you afraid of developing close relationships with others? Are you constantly harassed by evil spirits or felt that sin and Satan has taken control of your life? Are you partaking in occult practices and idol worship? Each of the aforementioned situations requires deliverance. Now that you are aware of the situations that can spiritually imprison you, it's time to experience your deliverance.

Knowing your promises in Christ is the only way you can be delivered. However, victory over the enemy can only occur by knowing against whom and what you are fighting. Your best defense mechanism against the enemy is having a thorough understanding of the strategy and weaponry that will be used against you. Sun Tzu, a Chinese general and author of the *Art of War* from circa 500 B.C., is the most quoted Chinese writer today. His advice "know your enemy" is followed by many military leaders around the world. Do not fight against an unknown enemy. Learn all you can before you go into battle. Know that you can win first. Apostle Paul said to Timothy: "This charge I commit to you, son Timothy, according to the prophecies previously made concerning you, that by them you may wage the good warfare" (1 Timothy 1:18). We are born into a spiritual war zone, and God invites us to be born again into His army to fight our way to heaven.

**Types of Spirits**

There are many spirits that are in rampage seeking to enter and destroy people's bodies, but let me focus on three types of spirits that can possess your body, soul, and spirit: seducing or deceiving spirits, unclean spirits, and spirits of infirmities.

## Seducing or Deceiving Spirits

"Now the Spirit expressly says that in latter times some will depart from the faith, giving heed to deceiving spirits and doctrines of demons" (1 Timothy 4:1). Seducing spirits control your conscience through enticement, temptation, fascination, arousal, and deception. These spirits emerge through false doctrine, cults, false teachers, fortune tellers, witches, palm readers, and tea leaf readers. "Now it happened, as we went to prayer, that a certain slave girl possessed with a spirit of divination met us, who brought her masters much profit by fortune-telling" (Acts 16:16). Using unscriptural methods, the spirit of divination foretells your future by providing you with information about your life which is naturally unknown. The Bible warns us about familiar spirits. Leviticus 19:31 says, "Give no regard to mediums and familiar spirits; do not seek after them, to be defiled by them: I am the Lord your God."

## Unclean Spirits

Mark 5:2 says, "And when He had come out of the boat, immediately there met Him out of the tombs a man with an unclean spirit." During Jesus' time, unclean spirits were one of the most common problems He faced. These problems are still prevalent today, and evidence of such occurrences can be seen in our homes and family life. Unclean means foul, dirty, filthy, defiled or morally lewd. People with unclean spirits spew filth and lewdness from their mouths. Furthermore, they appear to be clean externally, but are actually foul and dirty internally.

People controlled by unclean spirits become a slave to Satan's deceptive strategies, which lead them into immoral activities. With such strategies, Satan can dominate homes, churches, and nations, thus allowing him to take control of multiple aspects of society. Examples of unclean spirits can be seen in the following scriptures:

"And when He had called His twelve disciples to Him, He gave them power over unclean spirits, to cast them out, and to heal all kinds of sickness and all kinds of disease" (Matthew 10:1).

"When an unclean spirit goes out of a man, he goes through dry places, seeking rest, and finds none" (Matthew 12:43).

"Now there was a man in their synagogue with an unclean spirit. And he cried out, saying, 'Let us alone! What have we to do with You, Jesus of Nazareth? Did You come to destroy us? I know who You are—the Holy One of God!" But Jesus rebuked him, saying, "Be quiet, and come out of him!' And when the unclean spirit had convulsed him and cried out with a loud voice, he came out of him" (Mark 1:23-26).

"So I said: 'Woe is me, for I am undone! Because I am a man of unclean lips, and I dwell in the midst of a people of unclean lips; for my eyes have seen the King, The Lord of hosts'" (Isaiah 6:5).

Unclean spirits exist in every aspect of our daily life. You may be looking at a morally acceptable show on television, and then suddenly during a commercial break, immoral advertisements may start bombarding your television screen. Or you may be driving on a highway with your family when your eyes suddenly catch onto a lewd billboard display. Despite these distractions, you must obey Philippians 4:8: "Finally, brethren, whatever things are true, whatever things are noble, whatever things are just, whatever things are pure, whatever things are lovely, whatever things are of good report, if there is any virtue and if there is anything praiseworthy—meditate on these things."

Unclean spirits thrive in unclean places. Take for instance Jesus commanding the unclean spirits to come out of the demon-possessed man. Upon Jesus' command, the unclean spirits requested that He allow them to take up residence in the herd of swine, which are well-known for their unclean nature.

For He said to him, "Come out of the man, unclean spirit!" Then He asked him, "What is your name?" And he answered, saying, "My name is Legion; for we are many." Also, he begged Him earnestly that He would not send them out of the country. Now a large herd of swine was feeding there near the mountains. So all the demons begged Him, saying, "Send us to the swine, that we may enter them." And at once Jesus gave them permission. Then the unclean spirits went out and entered the swine (there were about two thousand); and the herd ran violently down the steep place into the sea, and drowned in the sea (Mark 5:8-13).

When you allow filthiness in your life, you send an invitation for unclean spirits to take up residence. Avoid using foul language and associating yourself with unclean people. These associations will only establish you as a potential habitation for an unclean spirit. Once the unclean spirit takes control, its residency reaches to a point where you are unable to escape the bondage of uncleanness. The demon-possessed man could break chains and fetters, but not the grip of the unclean spirits that had him bound in his foul sin. If he hadn't met Jesus, he would have died in that awful state.

Jesus can still rescue people who have unclean spirits. He had the power when He walked among men, and He has the same power today. It is still possible for someone to be born again and become a new creature in Christ. We do not see it happening a lot because the Gospel is often weak and watered down, but it is still possible for people to forsake their filthy state and become clean. The blood of Christ still washes white as snow, and when a person believes and obeys the absolute truth of God's Word, he will have dominion over unclean spirits. "Therefore, since all these things will be dissolved, what manner of persons ought you to be in holy conduct and godliness" (2 Peter 3:11). "You are already clean because of the word which I have spoken to you" (John 15:3).

## Spirits of Infirmities

These spirits afflict the bodies of Christians and non-Christians. In Luke 13:10-17, Jesus healed a woman from the spirit of infirmity. This woman was present during one of Jesus' teachings on the Sabbath and He referred to her as "a daughter of Abraham." This story indicates that this woman served God; however, she had been held under spiritual bondage by Satan for eighteen years.

> Now He was teaching in one of the synagogues on the Sabbath. And behold, there was a woman who had a spirit of infirmity eighteen years, and was bent over and could in no way raise herself up. But when Jesus saw her, He called her to Him and said to her, "Woman, you are loosed from your infirmity." And He laid His hands on her, and immediately she was made straight, and glorified God. But the ruler of the synagogue answered with indignation, because Jesus had healed on the Sabbath; and he said to the crowd, "There are six days on which men ought to work; therefore, come and be healed on them, and not on the Sabbath day." The Lord then answered him and said, "Hypocrite! Does not each one of you on the Sabbath loose his ox or donkey from the stall, and lead it away to water it? So ought not this woman, being a daughter of Abraham, whom Satan has bound—think of it—for eighteen years, be loosed from this bond on the Sabbath?" And when He said these things, all His adversaries were put to shame; and all the multitude rejoiced for all the glorious things that were done by Him (Luke 13:10-17).

Take a look through the Bible and you will see that the term "spirit of infirmity" is rarely used. There is only one time that the Bible uses the term. It appears in Luke 13:11, where it says, "And behold, there was a woman who had a spirit of infirmity eighteen years, and was bent over and could in no way raise herself up."

Although the term "spirit of infirmity" is widely used today, it does not carry the same weight as the one used in Luke 13:11. Presently, the "spirit of infirmity" represents demons that afflict people with sickness. Since the term carries different meanings for different people, I'll describe how I use it and the strategies that I adopt when praying for the sick. Let's take a look at two types of demonic illnesses. The first type of demon comes in the form of an illness. It dwells in its victim without any legitimate right and for whatever period of time it desires. Despite its freeloading nature, this demon can be easily removed from the afflicted person, since it does not have the authority to reside in that body. On the other hand, the second type of demon has permission to possess its victim. Such permission may be derived from ancestral sins, soul ties or ritual curses. Both of these demons will not depart from the afflicted person until they are commanded to do so. While the freeloading demon is easier to cast out, the demon with the legitimate right tends to put up a greater fight to extend the period of time under which it will hold its victim in bondage. Casting out the second type of demon is an extensive process.

# Chapter Two:
# Deception of the Enemy

"But I fear, lest somehow, as the serpent deceived Eve by his craftiness, so your minds may be corrupted from the simplicity that is in Christ."

2 Corinthians 11:3

Satan has a plan and he works this plan through the world as mentioned in 1 John 5:19: "We know that we are children of God, and that the whole world lies under the sway of the wicked one." As the prince of this world, Satan, influences people, especially those in authority." In Revelation 20:3, He is described as a "deceiver of nations." Satan Knows that he has a limited amount of time and his mission is to deceive as many people as possible. Revelation 20:7-8 says, "And he cast him into the bottomless pit, and shut him up, and set a seal on him, so that he should deceive the nations no more till the thousand years were finished. But after these things he must be released for a little while . . . Now when the thousand years have expired, Satan will be released from his prison and will go out to deceive the nations which are in the four corners of the earth, Gog and Magog, to gather them together to battle, whose number is as the sand of the sea." Satan is like a roaring lion in the world according to 1 Peter 5:8: "Be sober, be vigilant, because your adversary the devil walks about like a roaring lion, seeking whom he may devour."

Satan works both openly and secretly in the world, and his activities are always directed against God, His plan, and His people. This is quite evident in his rebellion and fall from Heaven, which occurs in Ezekiel 28:12-19.

"Son of man, take up a lamentation for the king of Tyre, and say to him, 'Thus says the Lord God:

"You were the seal of perfection,
Full of wisdom and perfect in beauty.
You were in Eden, the garden of God;
Every precious stone was your covering:
The sardius, topaz, and diamond,
Beryl, onyx, and jasper,
Sapphire, turquoise, and emerald with gold.
The workmanship of your timbrels and pipes
Was prepared for you on the day you were created.
"You were the anointed cherub who covers;
I established you;
You were on the holy mountain of God;
You walked back and forth in the midst of fiery stones.
You were perfect in your ways from the day you were created,
Till iniquity was found in you.
"By the abundance of your trading
You became filled with violence within,
And you sinned;
Therefore, I cast you as a profane thing
Out of the mountain of God;
And I destroyed you, O covering cherub,
From the midst of the fiery stones.
"Your heart was lifted up because of your beauty;
You corrupted your wisdom for the sake of your splendor;
I cast you to the ground,
I laid you before kings,
That they might gaze at you.
"You defiled your sanctuaries
By the multitude of your iniquities,
By the iniquity of your trading;
Therefore, I brought fire from your midst;
It devoured you,
And I turned you to ashes upon the earth
In the sight of all who saw you.
All who knew you among the peoples are astonished at you;
You have become a horror,
And shall be no more forever" (Ezekiel 28:12-19).

Satan opposed the work of Jesus when he came to this earth. He supports the "anti-Christ" spirit of the world and opposes the work of the Holy Spirit in the world. One purpose of the Holy Spirit is to guide you into the truth of the Word of God. Hence, Satan tries to keep the Word of God from influencing the hearts and lives of men and women. He encourages a love of the world in your heart, which is why the Bible says according to 1 John 2:15-16: "Do not love the world or the things in the world. If anyone loves the world, the love of the Father is not in him. For all that is in the world—the lust of the flesh, the lust of the eyes, and the pride of life—is not of the Father but is of the world."

Satan has a way of deceiving you and that is through "spiritual wickedness in high places." This is his mode of operation in the religious sector of the world. He deceives people through false doctrine, ministers, teachers, apostles, and religions. Moreover, Satan wages warfare against you as a believer who is in, but not of, the world.

> Finally, my brethren, be strong in the Lord and in the power of His might. Put on the whole armor of God that you may be able to stand against the wiles of the devil. For we do not wrestle against flesh and blood, but against principalities, against powers, against the rulers of the darkness of this age, against spiritual hosts of wickedness in the heavenly places. Therefore, take up the whole armor of God that you may be able to withstand in the evil day, and having done all, to stand. Stand, therefore, having girded your waist with truth, having put on the breastplate of righteousness, and having shod your feet with the preparation of the gospel of peace; above all, taking the shield of faith with which you will be able to quench all the fiery darts of the wicked one. And take the helmet of salvation, and the sword of the Spirit, which is the word of God; praying always with all prayer and supplication in the Spirit, being watchful to this end with all perseverance and supplication for all the saints (Ephesians 6:10-18).

Satan accuses and slanders you as a believer by planting doubt in your mind. An illustration of such deception is the first temptation of man in the Garden of Eden in Genesis 3:1-5.

"Now the serpent was more cunning than any beast of the field which the Lord God had made. And he said to the woman, "Has God indeed said, 'You shall not eat of every tree of the garden?'" And the woman said to the serpent, "We may eat the fruit of the trees of the garden, but of the fruit of the tree which is in the midst of the garden, God has said, 'You shall not eat it, nor shall you touch it, lest you die.'" Then the serpent said to the woman, "You will not surely die. For God knows that in the day you eat of it, your eyes will be opened, and you will be like God, knowing good and evil" (Genesis 3:1-5).

Satan wars against your mind, tongue, spirit, body, and spiritual walls, launching attacks against you through your family, associates, finances, and circumstances. The body, soul, and spirit of man are closely related. Due to this relationship, Satan accesses the soul and spirit through the flesh. This strategy is evident in the first temptation of man. Eve saw that "the tree was good for food and it was pleasant to the eyes, and a tree to be desired to make one wise. Therefore, she took of it and also gave it to her husband" (Genesis 3:6). Satan used fleshly senses and desires to gain access to Eve's soul and spirit. If Satan cannot "blind your mind" and keep you from accepting the truth of the Gospel, he will attempt to keep you as a prisoner to the flesh. Fleshly lusts war against the soul. In 1 Peter 2:11, the Bible says, "Beloved, I beg you as sojourners and pilgrims, abstain from fleshly lusts which war against the soul."

Satan uses the flesh to influence your mind and spirit, thus leading your life onto a pathway of corruption (rottenness and perversion). In Ephesians 4 where Paul deals with the sins of the flesh in the context of the old man and the new man, he warns us in verse 27 "nor gives place to the devil." This warning indicates that when you commit these fleshly sins, you allow Satan to have a claim over your life. Continuous willful indulgence in fleshly sins can result in captivity to Satan.

*Ambush the Enemy*

Demonic spirits are another medium through which Satan works. He takes charge of your life by gaining access to your body, soul, and spirit. When you are born again, you cannot be possessed by Satan, as long as you remain a true believer and stay under the covering of the blood of Jesus Christ. However, as a believer you may engage in consistent fleshly sins that eventually transform from a sin of the flesh into a sin controlled by demonic activity.

The world, the flesh, and the devil with his demons combine their evil forces to war against you as a child of God. Each force can operate independently against you, but these forces of evil are most often unified in their attack upon your life. Here are some powerful scriptural counterstrategies for overcoming these forces. The Bible says present your body as a sacrifice. In the military force of the natural world, a man who enlists for service comes under the complete control of his superiors. They give him instructions on how to conduct himself, how to dress, and how to fight the enemy. In order to be effective in spiritual warfare, the same type of control must be put into action. In Romans 12:1-2, Paul says, "I beseech you, therefore, brethren, by the mercies of God, that you present your bodies a living sacrifice, holy, acceptable to God, which is your reasonable service. And do not be conformed to this world, but be transformed by the renewing of your mind, that you may prove what is that good and acceptable and perfect will of God."

You must present yourself to God as an act of your own will. In the Old Testament when a sacrifice was given to God, the person who offered it had no further control over it. It was given totally to the Lord. Instead of conforming to the world and the flesh, you must be transformed (changed) by the renewing of your mind. It is imperative that you arm yourself with the mind of Christ. In 1 Peter 4:1-2, the Bible says, "Therefore, since Christ suffered for us in the flesh, arm yourselves also with the same mind, for he who has suffered in the flesh has ceased from sin, that he no longer should live the rest of his time in the flesh for the lusts of men, but for the will of God." The renewing of your mind is done by "arming" yourself with the same mind as Jesus. Develop a proper attitude toward your flesh. We are told that we should "hate even the garment spotted by the flesh" in Jude 1:23. The lust of the flesh is not of the Father, but of the world. Therefore, you should have no confidence in the flesh.

Life in the flesh brings about corruption, while life in the spirit brings about vitality. Come to a place in your life where you realize you do not have to be in bondage to the flesh. In the past, you were a prisoner to the flesh when you were a sinner. Ephesians 2 says:

> And you He made alive, who were dead in trespasses and sins, in which you once walked according to the course of this world, according to the prince of the power of the air, the spirit who now works in the sons of disobedience, among whom also we all once conducted ourselves in the lusts of our flesh, fulfilling the desires of the flesh and of the mind, and were by nature children of wrath, just as the others.
>
> But God, who is rich in mercy, because of His great love with which He loved us, even when we were dead in trespasses, made us alive together with Christ (by grace you have been saved), and raised us up together, and made us sit together in the heavenly places in Christ Jesus, that in the ages to come He might show the exceeding riches of His grace in His kindness toward us in Christ Jesus. For by grace you have been saved through faith, and that not of yourselves; it is the gift of God, not of works, lest anyone should boast. For we are His workmanship, created in Christ Jesus for good works, which God prepared beforehand that we should walk in them.
>
> Therefore, remember that you, once Gentiles in the flesh—who are called Uncircumcision by what is called the Circumcision made in the flesh by hands—that at that time you were without Christ, being aliens from the commonwealth of Israel and strangers from the covenants of promise, having no hope and without God in the world. But now in Christ Jesus you who once were far off have been brought near by the blood of Christ.

For He Himself is our peace, who has made both one, and has broken down the middle wall of separation, having abolished in His flesh the enmity, that is, the law of commandments contained in ordinances, so as to create in Himself one new man from the two, thus making peace, and that He might reconcile them both to God in one body through the cross, thereby putting to death the enmity. And He came and preached peace to you who were afar off and to those who were near. For through Him we both have access by one Spirit to the Father. Now, therefore, you are no longer strangers and foreigners, but fellow citizens with the saints and members of the household of God, having been built on the foundation of the apostles and prophets, Jesus Christ Himself being the chief cornerstone, in whom the whole building, being fitted together, grows into a holy temple in the Lord, in whom you also are being built together for a dwelling place of God in the Spirit.

Romans 8 says:

Therefore there is now no condemnation to those who are in Christ Jesus, who do not walk according to the flesh, but according to the Spirit. For the law of the Spirit of life in Christ Jesus has made me free from the law of sin and death. For what the law could not do in that it was weak through the flesh, God did by sending His own Son in the likeness of sinful flesh, on account of sin: He condemned sin in the flesh, that the righteous requirement of the law might be fulfilled in us who do not walk according to the flesh but according to the Spirit. For those who live according to the flesh set their minds on the things of the flesh, but those who live according to the Spirit, the things of the Spirit. For to be carnally minded is death, but to be spiritually minded is life and peace. Because the carnal mind is enmity against God, for it is not subject to the law of God, nor indeed can be. So then, those who are in the flesh cannot please God.

But you are not in the flesh but in the Spirit, if indeed the Spirit of God dwells in you. Now if anyone does not have the Spirit of

Christ, he is not His. And if Christ is in you, the body is dead because of sin, but the Spirit is life because of righteousness. But if the Spirit of Him who raised Jesus from the dead dwells in you, He who raised Christ from the dead will also give life to your mortal bodies through His Spirit who dwells in you.

Therefore, brethren, we are debtors—not to the flesh, to live according to the flesh. For if you live according to the flesh, you will die, but if by the Spirit you put to death the deeds of the body, you will live. For as many as are led by the Spirit of God, these are sons of God. For you did not receive the spirit of bondage again to fear, but you received the Spirit of adoption by whom we cry out, "Abba, Father." The Spirit Himself bears witness with our spirit that we are children of God, and if children, then heirs—heirs of God and joint heirs with Christ, if indeed we suffer with Him, that we may also be glorified together.

For I consider that the sufferings of this present time are not worthy to be compared with the glory which shall be revealed in us. For the earnest expectation of the creation eagerly waits for the revealing of the sons of God. For the creation was subjected to futility, not willingly, but because of Him who subjected it in hope; because the creation itself also will be delivered from the bondage of corruption into the glorious liberty of the children of God. For we know that the whole creation groans and labors with birth pangs together until now. Not only that, but we also who have the first fruits of the Spirit, even we ourselves groan within ourselves, eagerly waiting for the adoption, the redemption of our body. For we were saved in this hope, but hope that is seen is not hope, for why does one still hope for what he sees? But if we hope for what we do not see, we eagerly wait for it with perseverance.

Likewise, the Spirit also helps in our weaknesses. For we do not know what we should pray for as we ought, but the Spirit Himself makes intercession for us with groaning, which cannot be uttered. Now He who searches the hearts knows what the mind of the Spirit is, because He makes intercession for the saints according to the will of God. And we know that all things work together for good to those who love God, to those who are the called according to His purpose. For whom He foreknew, He also predestined to be conformed to the image of His Son, that He might be the firstborn among many brethren. Moreover whom He predestined, these He also called; whom He called, these He also justified; and whom He justified, and these He also glorified.

What then shall we say to these things? If God is for us, who can be against us? He who did not spare His own Son, but delivered Him up for us all, how shall He not with Him also freely give us all things? Who shall bring a charge against God's elect? It is God who justifies. Who is he who condemns? It is Christ who died, and furthermore is also risen, who is even at the right hand of God, who also makes intercession for us. Who shall separate us from the love of Christ? Shall tribulation, or distress, or persecution, or famine, or nakedness, or peril, or sword? As it is written:

"For Your sake we are killed all day long;
We are accounted as sheep for the slaughter."

Yet in all these things, we are more than conquerors through Him who loved us. For I am persuaded that neither death nor life, nor angels nor principalities nor powers, nor things present nor things to come, nor height nor depth, nor any other created thing, shall be able to separate us from the love of God which is in Christ Jesus our Lord.

You will discover you no longer have to be in captivity to the flesh. Your freedom comes through Jesus Christ. Train your flesh to obey. The Bible says obedience is better than sacrifice. In the military world, the soldier must obey all orders. He goes through basic training to learn the rules of warfare and participates in trial sessions where he must put these strategies into action, thus allowing him to learn through failure and success.

Such training also applies to the spiritual world. You must train your flesh to obey and learn God's rules. Through the trials that God permits in your life, you will have the opportunity to put these rules into action. Your training entails the study of your warfare manual, the Bible. I recommend the Robin Healing Ministries *Article of War for Spiritual Warfare Deliverance Bible*. As you exercise or train your spiritual senses, you will learn to discern between good and evil. Train your flesh to obey God's Word by taking the following action steps:

- Abstain from fleshly lusts.
- Cleanse yourself of filthiness of the flesh.
- Do not make provisions for the flesh.
- Put off the old man.

The "old man" refers to the flesh nature. Paul writes in Ephesians 4:22-24 "that you put off, concerning your former conduct, the old man which grows corrupt according to the deceitful lusts, and be renewed in the spirit of your mind, and that you put on the new man which was created according to God, in true righteousness and holiness." The flesh will not die a natural death. You must crucify it by refusing to be under its control.

Walking in the spirit means allowing God's Holy Spirit to control your life. The flesh does not have more power than the spirit. If you let the Holy Spirit manifest His power in you, it will quicken your mortal body of flesh. "Quicken" refers to the renewal of life. You do not have to live in the death of sin. God can quicken your spirit to new life. For you to be led by the spirit, you must have the Holy Spirit within you. You must be born again by the Spirit. John 3:6-7 says, "That which is born of the flesh is flesh, and that which is born of the Spirit is spirit. Do not marvel that I said to you, 'You must be born again.'"

You must also be filled with the Holy Spirit. It is the Holy Spirit who gives you power to walk in the spirit rather than the flesh. I cannot emphasize enough the importance of the Holy Spirit in overcoming the world, the flesh, and the devil. Let your spirit speak through the Holy Spirit. God communicates with your spirit through the Holy Spirit. Furthermore, the Holy Spirit communicates directly with God via your spirit. When you speak in an unknown language, which is the physical evidence of the baptism of the Holy Spirit according to Acts 2:1-4, your spirit is communicating directly with God. When this happens, it is important that you allow the Holy Spirit to function in its full capacity by praying according to the will of God.

> When the Day of Pentecost had fully come, they were all with one accord in one place. And suddenly there came a sound from heaven, as of a rushing mighty wind, and it filled the whole house where they were sitting. Then there appeared to them divided tongues, as of fire, and one sat upon each of them. And they were all filled with the Holy Spirit and began to speak with other tongues, as the Spirit gave them utterance (Acts 2:1-4).

Reject the works of the flesh and develop the fruit of the Holy Spirit: love, joy, peace, longsuffering, gentleness, goodness, faith, meekness, and temperance. Stop living in condemnation. Satan uses the weaknesses of the flesh to make you live in condemnation. However, Paul said in Romans 8:1, "There is therefore now no condemnation to those who are in Christ Jesus, who do not walk according to the flesh, but according to the Spirit." If you have been engaged in fleshly conduct, do not remain in condemnation. Repent and ask for forgiveness.

**Here are six ways to experience deliverance and become an overcomer:**

**Develop a proper attitude toward your surroundings.**

I will make them and the places all around My hill a blessing, and I will cause showers to come down in their season; there shall be showers of blessing (Ezekiel 34:26).

**Understand that you will experience attack from the devil.**

The thief does not come except to steal, and to kill, and to destroy. I have come that they may have life, and that they may have *it* more abundantly (John 10:10).

**Realize that gaining the world is not worth losing your soul.**

For what profit is it to a man if he gains the whole world, and loses his own soul? Or what will a man give in exchange for his soul? (Matthew 16:26).

**Realize that if you love the world, you are an enemy of God.**

Adulterers and adulteresses! Do you not know that friendship with the world is enmity with God? Whoever therefore wants to be a friend of the world makes himself an enemy of God (James 4:4).

**Recognize the temporal nature of the world.**

But this I say, brethren, the time *is* short, so that from now on even those who have wives should be as though they had none, [30] those who weep as though they did not weep, those who rejoice as though they did not rejoice, those who buy as though they did not possess, [31] and those who use this world as not misusing *it*. For the form of this world is passing away (1 Corinthians 7:29-31).

**Recognize you are not in spiritual bondage anymore.**

Stand fast therefore in the liberty by which Christ has made us free, and do not be entangled again with a yoke of bondage (Galatians 5:1).

As a believer, you do not have to be in bondage. Romans 12:1-3 says, "I beseech you, therefore, brethren, by the mercies of God, that you present your bodies a living sacrifice, holy, acceptable to God, which is your reasonable service. And do not be conformed to this world, but be transformed by the renewing of your mind, that you may prove what is that good and acceptable and perfect will of God. For I say, through the grace given to me, to everyone who is among you, not to think of himself more highly than he ought to think, but to think soberly, as God has dealt to each one a measure of faith." This means you are no longer conformed to the world. You are now a resident of the Kingdom of God. You are no longer under the power of the world. Now that you are free from the world, set a guard against its influence in your life. Do not pattern your life after the rudiments of the world.

It is very important that you understand your purpose and mission in life so that you are not affected by the world or the things of this world, but rather you influence the world through the word of your testimony and the power of the blood of Jesus Christ. You should be a light in a world of darkness, reflecting the glory of God and sharing the good news of the Gospel. The impact of the early believers on the world was so great that it was said of them that they "turned the world upside down." Acts 17:6 says, "But when they did not find them, they dragged Jason and some brethren to the rulers of the city, crying out, 'These who have turned the world upside down have come here, too.'"

# Chapter Three:
# Spiritual Strategies Against You

"Be sober; be vigilant; because your adversary the devil walks about like a roaring lion, seeking whom he may devour. Resist him, steadfast in the faith, knowing that the same sufferings are experienced by your brotherhood in the world."

1 Peter 5:8-9

The enemy has a very powerful strategy operating against you. He blinds your mind to the Gospel and snatches away the truth of the Gospel when you hear it. As a result, the Gospel sounds foolish and irrelevant to those who are lost in sin. In 1 Corinthians 1:18, the Bible says, "For the message of the cross is foolishness to those who are perishing, but to us who are being saved, it is the power of God." Satan also snares many non-Christians in false religions and leads them to walk according to the "course of the world," which is the philosophy of the age. This philosophy may vary from generation to generation and culture to culture, but it is always use flesh or man-centered rather than God-centered. Satan is constantly sowing the seeds of rebellion (sin) in the hearts and minds of unbelievers. One of the purposes of the Holy Spirit is to war against Satan for the souls of unbelievers. That is why God gave us the Holy Spirit because it works to convict men and women of their rebellion against God. In John 16:7-11, the Bible says, "Nevertheless, I tell you the truth. It is to your advantage that I go away; for if I do not go away, the Helper will not come to you; but if I depart, I will send Him to you. And when He has come, He will convict the world of sin, and of righteousness, and of judgment: of sin, because they do not believe in Me; of righteousness, because I go to My Father and you see Me no more; of judgment, because the ruler of this world is judged."

When you accept Jesus Christ as your Lord and Savior, it certainly does not mean the battle is over. You have won one major confrontation when you are saved, but in reality, your intense struggle has only begun. You will learn many strategies of Satan as you continue to study the word of God. These strategies will arm you with spiritual weapons and prepare you to enter the enemy's territory. Here are four major areas in your life where Satan will attack:

**The Word of God**: Satan will cause you to question the Word of God and will add to, take from, or distort the scriptures. This is what happened in the very first temptation with Eve. That is why it is important for you to study and understand God's Word so you will not be deceived by such attacks.

**Your Worship to God**: Satan's original rebellion involved his desire to be worshiped. Hence the reason, he targets Christian's worship to God. His goal is to lead you into false or fleshly worship, thus preventing you from worshipping God wholeheartedly.

**Your Walk with God**: Satan causes slander and tempts you to engage in the works of the flesh. Under this satanic influence, you will become occupied with the world. With Satan in control of your life, you will rely upon your own human wisdom and strength. If Satan can win territory in your personal walk with God, it will make it easier for him to prevent you from carrying out God's assignment for your life.

**Your Work for God**: Satan will try to deter you from accomplishing God's will through persecution, disaster, discouragement, prayerlessness, and extensive involvement with the cares of the world. Additionally, he will attempt to affect your work for God by infiltrating the church with false teachers and disciples. Matthew 13:38-39 says, "The field is the world, the good seeds are the sons of the kingdom, but the tares are the sons of the wicked one. The enemy who sowed them is the devil, the harvest is the end of the age, and the reapers are the angels." While God sows good seed through your life, the enemy sows tares which are the "sons of the wicked one." Satan promotes division within the Body of Christ by trying to affect the work of God and His purpose in your life.

Besides mind control, Satan uses your family as another means of gaining control over you. Take for instance, you may have a child using drugs, a teenage daughter becoming pregnant, or a spouse being unfaithful or filing for divorce. Such attacks and problems are occurring regularly in families around the world. Although the attack came to fruition today, the sequence of events leading up to the final outcome may have been present for several months or years in your life.

Blessings take place in your life when God allows a person to enter your life for that specific purpose. Likewise, when the enemy wants to obstruct your life, he will use someone to reap that destruction. Therefore, it is essential that you discern people. I will share more on how to discern in another chapter of this book. For now, remember that when you develop relationships through work or ministry, it is important to have a deeper understanding of the persons with whom you interact. Sometimes, we may have good days and bad days. However, when people have a true relationship with you, they will understand such scenarios and they will not judge you due to the dismal mode in which you may be operating on a specific day. During these moments, people may react due to their dismal circumstances and will have to apologize to the person who was offended. You must always be willing to apologize if you are the one in the wrong. Satan can use anyone to say the wrong things to trigger confusion, even good people. It may not be what you say, but how it is said.

Take a look at the time when Jesus warned His disciples about His crucifixion and ascension. Peter admonished Jesus, who in turn rebuked him. The Bible says, "But He turned and said to Peter, "Get behind Me, Satan! You are an offense to Me, for you are not mindful of the things of God, but the things of men" (Matthew 16:23). In Matthew 16:16-17, Peter had spoken a great revelation about Jesus. Simon Peter answered and said, "You are the Christ, the Son of the living God." Jesus answered and said to him, "Blessed are you, Simon

Bar-Jonah, for flesh and blood has not revealed this to you, but My Father who is in heaven." What changed? When Jesus was telling Peter about His suffering, Peter believed that he had received another revelation. Then Peter took Him aside and began to rebuke Him, saying, "Far be it from You, Lord; this shall not happen to You!" (Matthew 16:22). When Peter spoke out of context, it did not happen because he was against the Lord. The problem stems from the fact that Peter was speaking in opposition to God's will in contrast to the revelation from God which he had spoken earlier.

Let's get back to the subject of how the enemy uses others to destroy you. The real battle is against the truth. Whenever the enemy is coming against you with a temptation or a trial, what he is trying to do is seduce you away from the truth. As I mentioned before, a seducing spirit is a spirit of deception. The Greek word for seduce means "to cause to wonder or to lead astray or to seduce." It is close to the Greek word for wondering, as wondering in the wilderness without knowing your direction. The seducing spirit causes the mind to wander. As your mind wanders, you are influenced by a spirit of confusion. The Bible says, "You will keep him in perfect peace, whose mind is stayed on You, because he trusts in You" (Isaiah 26:3). If you will keep your mind on Him, He promises to give you perfect peace. In Hebrew, it says he will keep us in Shalom. Shalom is the Hebrew word for *peace*, but in translating to English, you cannot translate it peace-peace because it would look like a misprint. The literal translation peace-peace means that He will keep you in double peace. Your brain has two hemispheres, the left and the right, which control different areas of the body and different senses. God says that He will keep you in double peace, or surround you with peace so that both hemispheres of the mind will be at peace.

*Please note: (To **wander** is to move about with no destination or purpose. It is a physical activity; though the word is sometimes used figuratively for nonphysical actions that are aimless (e.g., a movie or a conversation might wander). To **wonder** is to feel curiosity, to be in doubt, or to have a feeling of admiration.*

The Hebrew Word for "stay" is like that of a pole of a tent where all the weight of the tent is on the pole. As long as the pole is steady and stayed in the right position, it can hold the weight of the tent. If you keep your mind *stayed*, the word of God resting on your mind, then God will keep your mind in perfect peace because you, like a tent, are stayed upon Him. Philippians 4:8 says, "Finally, brethren, whatever things are true, whatever things are noble, whatever things are just, whatever things are pure, whatever things are lovely, whatever things are of good report, if there is any virtue and if there is anything praiseworthy—meditate on these things."

Your depression comes when you get off-track and start worrying about things. Becoming fearful is simply worrying in advance. Most fears are not based on fact, but possibilities or speculation of what might or could happen that has no merit. Seducing spirits put pressure on an individual causing that person's mind to wander from the truth. You may be thinking about something and suddenly a fiery dart comes into your mind, where you find yourself totally distracted and thinking about things of the flesh. You must keep your mind stayed on God and His Word to defeat the seducing spirit.

If a person yields to a seducing spirit and does it long enough, it will first come to distort the truth, then pervert the truth and destroy it. In 1 Timothy 4:1-2, it says, "Now the Spirit expressly says that in latter times some will depart from the faith, giving heed to deceiving spirits and doctrines of demons, speaking lies in hypocrisy, having their own conscience seared with a hot iron." That searing of the conscience is connected to the seducing spirit. When the seducing spirit works against a person's mind, the individual begins to give into the seduction and lie, thus confusing the mind to the point where the person justifies the lie and sin.

Our conscience has the ability to determine between right and wrong. The word conscience means "to know with" and it is the part of the mind or soul that governs the knowledge that we receive in our life. This causes a battle in the thought life. Continual sin and disobedience to God debilitates a person's conscience to the point where determining right from wrong becomes nonexistent. People who fall into this category say: "Whatever religion you are is fine. There is no one way that is right or the only way, since they all lead to God." These deceptions are the end result of being deceived by a seducing spirit. Satan's master plan is to sear your conscience, thus preventing you from responding to the call of the Holy Spirit upon your life.

Genesis 6:3 says, "And the Lord said, 'My Spirit shall not strive with man forever, for he is indeed flesh; yet his days shall be one hundred and twenty years.'" This is the truth. The Holy Spirit will come and convict you if you have done something wrong. You will feel a burden and uneasiness until you make it right. As long as you have this conviction of the spirit, it demonstrates that you have some level of a relationship with God. This is the first way that God chastises us when we sin. He will let you know that your spirit is not right until you go back to the cross and repent. You don't get saved again, but you make your relationship right. With a true child of God, when you sin, you will be convicted and you will experience uneasiness in your spirit. You must be thankful for such an experience. If you ever get to the point where you can sin and not be convicted by it, then sin has debilitated your conscience and you are under the control of some form of a seducing spirit. Your conscience is an inner voice that speaks to you when you break God's laws. Yet today so many can do horrible things and have no remorse. Be careful of what you allow into your spirit.

The conscience can be seared when it is overloaded with many things. At first, you will be convicted and bothered by things. However, doing more of what you shouldn't practice only makes you become more immune to that lifestyle. Such behavior forces you to pay less attention to your conviction until you arrive in the danger zone where you are no longer affected by your wrongdoing. When I first came into the church in 1987, the members were very strict and believed in the separation from all the things belonging to the world because of their concern with displeasing the Lord and wrongly affecting their walk with Him. As a result, they were godly and holy which reflected through their lifestyle. They were different and the world knew it. They were mockingly called holy rollers. Nowadays, you cannot distinguish between the church and the world. The latter does not respect the church, but rather mocks its practices.

You must understand that your flesh is evil by nature and is against the things of God. In order to live right and do right, it is imperative that you connect with God and separate yourself from the things of the world. The world may view your stance as absurd, and that is because they cannot understand the things of God. For you to keep your conscience from being seared, you must learn to be sensitive to the Holy Spirit. Sanctify yourself from the filthiness of the flesh and perfect holiness in the sight of God. Seeking more of God's presence in your life requires you to lay aside more of the flesh and world. Today, many speak of desiring God's glory to fall on them. However, if it did, they would probably not have the strength to contain it because you cannot go into God's presence with sin and continue along that sinful path. Think of the High Priest going into the presence of God without first being cleansed.

For you to experience freedom in your walk with God, you must be willing to lay aside anything for which the Holy Spirit convicts you. If you do not, the very thing you do not lay aside could become a snare to you. God may even ask something of you or ask you not to do something that you see other Christians doing. Do not question the Holy Spirit and what is placed in your heart. The other people are not your servant nor are you theirs, but the Lord's. You do not have to look at others or what they do, but focus on what God wants for you.

Things that others do may not be a problem for them; however, such practices could place you in bondage. You are not the Lord and neither am I. You must work out your own salvation with fear and trembling as it says in Philippians 2:12: "Therefore, my beloved, as you have always obeyed, not as in my presence only, but now much more in my absence, work out your own salvation with fear and trembling." We each have an individual walk before the Lord. In John 10:27, it says, "My sheep hear My voice, and I know them, and they follow Me." Some things that godly people do, the Lord may not allow you to do. I am not talking about sin. Sin is sin to everyone. Yet there is a place where we must walk by faith before the Lord for ourselves. Do not worry about what others think, but what the Lord thinks. Do not worry about pleasing men, but the Lord. People may laugh at or misunderstand you because of your choice to do what the Lord requires of you rather than what they would like you to do. The question is, what can you do? Satan uses various powerful strategies as he works against you and God. It is very important to study the enemy, the spiritual forces of evil, the enemy's territory and his strategy so that you are equipped for the battle.

# Chapter Four:
# Standing Against Spiritual Forces

"For we do not wrestle against flesh and blood, but against principalities, against powers, against the rulers of the darkness of this age, against spiritual hosts of wickedness in the heavenly places."

Ephesians 6:12

When the enemy is coming against you, you can expose its attack by carrying your burden to the Lord by praying in the Holy Spirit and entering into spiritual warfare. Always be careful not to confuse how you feel during your battle with depression as such feelings may only be a burden that the Lord placed in your heart. When God places a burden in your spirit, it is time to pray. A burden from God is a signal of two things: a signal to pray or a signal to change because God is forewarning you that a major transformation is coming in your life, ministry, or church. It is only when your spirit is under heavy pressure that you can effectively say long prayers until the burden are released.

While carrying your burden, praying in the Holy Spirit and entering into spiritual warfare are effective strategies to expose the enemy; doing so before it happens is the best way of counteracting his plan against you. Do not wait until you are in battle to prepare. You can fend off an attack of Satan by praying in the Spirit. The most effective prayers when you are carrying a burden and you do not know what is happening, but you know that something is wrong or about to happen, are those prayed in the Holy Spirit. Allow the Holy Spirit to intercede for you and bring revelation to expose the attack before it comes like God did with Elijah. Even if you do not get a revelation, pray until the burden is lifted and you know that God has somehow intervene in the situation through your prayers in the Spirit.

God can supernaturally abort the plans of the enemy against you through prayer. Prayer can nullify and render an attack useless. History has shown us how a man by the name of Alexander the Great accomplished the impossible by taking over the world within ten years of entering the military. He defeated an army of one million with approximately 40,000 troops, losing about 500 men in contrast to his enemy's thousands. How? How was Alexander the Great able to pull off this defeat? He studied his enemy's weakness by carefully analyzing their defense and paying particular attention to any inconsistencies or unguarded walls in their strategy. Satan uses the same analysis in our lives. Hence the reason why it is essential that we develop a keen eye to identify such weaknesses in Satan's camp and capitalize on them.

When Alexander's men were about to go into battle, he lightened their load before battle. They could not carry weapons and baggage, so he had them remove all baggage before the war and appointed someone to watch the baggage while the war was in progress. His army was very light and quick on their feet in contrast to the other army. Paul said in 2 Timothy 2:4, "No one engaged in warfare entangles himself with the affairs of this life, that he may please him who enlisted him as a soldier." Also, Hebrews 12:1 says, "Therefore, we also, since we are surrounded by so great a cloud of witnesses, let us lay aside every weight, and the sin which so easily ensnares us, and let us run with endurance the race that is set before us." In this spiritual battle, you must lay aside the weight, the cares of this life and things that choke the word, causing you to become unfruitful. The apostles became too busy waiting on tables and decided to appoint seven men to fulfill those duties so that they could devote more time to prayer and the ministry of the word.

Apart from lightening their load, Alexander fed his men during the journey and prior to the war. Just as it is impossible to fight a natural war without energy, so it is when fighting spiritual battles. You can wear your physical body down until it affects your mind and spirit, thus allowing the enemy to gain easy access to consume and destroy you. When the people had listened to Jesus three days without eating, He did not send them away without food because they would faint on the way. On two separate occasions, Elijah was supernaturally fed by an angel. When David was running from King Saul, he stopped and ate the showbread from the tabernacle. When Jonathan got tired, he ate honey, without hearing his father's order. You cannot fight without being fed physically and spiritually. Do not wait until you get into the war to put the Word into you.

When Alexander allowed his men to rest, the Persians had their men marching for fourteen hours, which eventually wore them out. Alexander only moved his men seven miles in four days. He did not wear them down before battle. There must be physical, spiritual, and emotional rest before battle; physical rest for the body, emotional rest for the mind, and spiritual rest for the spirit. You can be more effective when rested. While some may require only five hours of sleep to be rejuvenated, others may require more. Just as it is important to have knowledge of the strategies you will implement during battle, so it is also to spend time alone relaxing and rejuvenating yourself. This preparation will strengthen you to continue until the battle ends. Pray in the Spirit consistently, and God will either expose the plan of Satan before it happens or He will show you a way to escape.

Spiritual warfare is very important to win any battle in the realm of the spirit. It is not a natural battle between flesh and blood. Because the Kingdom of Satan is a spiritual kingdom, this warfare must be fought in the Spirit. It is not a visible battle of man against man. Since Satan's kingdom is spiritual, this warfare must be fought in the Spirit. The Bible says, "For we wrestle not against flesh and blood, but against principalities, against powers, against the rulers of the darkness of this age, against spiritual wickedness in heavenly places" (Ephesians 6:12). Spiritual warfare is "multidimensional," which means that it is fought in different dimensions. Such dimensions consist of:

1. A social battle between the believer and the world.

    If the world hates you, you know that it hated Me before it hated you. If you were of the world, the world would love its own. Yet because you are not of the world, but I chose you out of the world; therefore, the world hates you. Remember the word that I said to you, 'A servant is not greater than his master.' If they persecuted Me, they will also persecute you. If they kept My word, they will keep yours also. But all these things they will do to you for My name's sake, because they do not know Him who sent Me. If I had not come and spoken to them, they would have no sin, but now they have no excuse for their sin. He who hates Me hates My Father also. If I had not done among them the works which no one else did, they would have no sin; but now they have seen and also hated both Me and My Father. But this happened that the word might be fulfilled, which is written in their law, 'They hated Me without a cause. But when the Helper comes, whom I shall send to you from the Father, the Spirit of truth who proceeds from the Father, He will testify of Me. And you also will bear witness, because you have been with Me from the beginning' (John 15:18-27).

2. A personal battle between the flesh and the spirit.

    I say then: Walk in the Spirit, and you shall not fulfill the lust of the flesh. For the flesh lusts against the Spirit and the Spirit against the flesh; and these are contrary to one another, so that you do not do the things that you wish. But if you are led by the Spirit, you are not under the law. Now the works of the flesh are evident, which are adultery, fornication, uncleanness, lewdness, idolatry, sorcery, hatred, contentions, jealousies, outbursts of wrath, selfish ambitions, dissensions, heresies, envy, murders, drunkenness, revelries, and the like; of which I tell you beforehand, just as I also told you in time past, that those who practice such things will not inherit the kingdom of God. But the fruit of the Spirit is love, joy, peace, longsuffering, kindness, goodness, faithfulness, gentleness, self-control. Against such there is no law. And those who are Christ's have crucified the flesh with its passions and desires. If we live in the Spirit, let us also walk in the Spirit. Let us not become conceited, provoking one another, envying one another (Galatians 5:16-26).

3. A supernatural battle between believers and evil spiritual powers.

Finally, my brethren, be strong in the Lord and in the power of His might. Put on the whole armor of God that you may be able to stand against the wiles of the devil. For we do not wrestle against flesh and blood, but against principalities, against powers, against the rulers of the darkness of this age, against spiritual hosts of wickedness in the heavenly places. Therefore, take up the whole armor of God that you may be able to withstand in the evil day, and having done all, to stand. Stand therefore, having girded your waist with truth, having put on the breastplate of righteousness, and having shod your feet with the preparation of the gospel of peace; above all, taking the shield of faith with which you will be able to quench all the fiery darts of the wicked one. And take the helmet of salvation, and the sword of the Spirit, which is the word of God; praying always with all prayer and supplication in the Spirit, being watchful to this end with all perseverance and supplication for all the saints—and for me, that utterance may be given to me, that I may open my mouth boldly to make known the mystery of the gospel, for which I am an ambassador in chains; that in it I may speak boldly, as I ought to speak. But that you also may know my affairs and how I am doing, Tychicus, a beloved brother and faithful minister in the Lord, will make all things known to you; whom I have sent to you for this very purpose, that you may know our affairs, and that he may comfort your hearts. Peace to the brethren, and love with faith, from God the Father and the Lord Jesus Christ. Grace be with all those who love our Lord Jesus Christ in sincerity. Amen (Ephesians 6:10-24).

Every person alive is engaged in this battle, whether that individual realizes it or not. There is no neutral ground. Unbelievers are victims of spiritual warfare who have been taken captive by enemy forces. While believers are victors who have been freed from the enemy through Jesus Christ, they are still engaged in spiritual warfare. The key verse in Ephesians 6 indicates that all believers wrestle against evil spiritual forces. "For we do not wrestle against flesh and blood, but against principalities, against powers, against the rulers of the darkness of this age, against spiritual hosts of wickedness in the heavenly places" (verse 12). "Wrestling" involves close personal contact. Therefore, no one is exempt from this battle. You are in the midst of conflict whether you acknowledge it or not. If you believe it will get better, you are wrong. Spiritual warfare never ceases.

Satan knows that the end is near, and he fights to maintain control of the kingdoms of the world. He does not want t people to come under God's authority. Hence the reason, the battle rages within the hearts, minds, and souls of men and women. Satan blinds the minds of unbelievers and attacks believers in the areas of worship, the Word, their daily walk, and their work for God.

Demonic spirits are agents that Satan uses to accomplish his purposes in people's lives. If you are seeking personal deliverance, you must learn how to deal with demonic powers that obsess, oppress, or possess the body, soul, and spirit. You may not be the only one who is tormented by a demonic spirit. There are many people around you who are tormented, troubled, and in some cases, possessed by the powers of darkness known as demons.

It is also very important for you to know how demonic spirits operate. Demonic spirits are used by Satan to oppose God, His plan and purposes, and His people. They also war against unbelievers to keep them from the truth of the Gospel. Demonic spirits control specific territories (principalities) such as the prince of Persia mentioned in Daniel 10:12-13. "Then he said to me, 'Do not fear, Daniel, for from the first day that you set your heart to understand, and to humble yourself before your God, your words were heard; and I have come because of your words. But the prince of the kingdom of Persia withstood me twenty-one days; and behold, Michael, one of the chief princes, came to help me, for I had been left alone there with the kings of Persia.'" They also work through personalities, through men and women, to accomplish satanic objectives in the world. Opposition to God's will is Satan's main objective. The word "Satan" means "adversary." Satan is primarily God's adversary and secondarily, man's adversary.

Demonic spirits have different natures. Remember that one demon identified himself in I Kings 22:22 as a "lying spirit." The Lord said to him, 'In what way?' So he said, 'I will go out and be a lying spirit in the mouth of all his prophets.' And the Lord said, 'You shall persuade him, and also prevail. Go out and do so.'" A "deaf and dumb" spirit is identified in Mark 9:25. "When Jesus saw that the people came running together, He rebuked the unclean spirit, saying to it: 'Deaf and dumb spirit, I command you, come out of him and enter him no more" Demons of various natures operate as spirits of infirmity, seducing spirits, and unclean spirits. Satan uses them to war against man in body, soul, and spirit. I know you may be asking the question, "Is it a demonic spirit that possesses someone if they are deaf and dumb?" The answer is yes, they are possessed with a demonic spirit.

Demons love to possess or reside in human beings. Demon possession is a condition in which one or more evil spirits (demons) inhabit the body of a person and take complete control of their victim at will. Some people prefer using the word "demonized" rather than possession, but regardless of the term, the possessed person becomes a host in which demons reside. "Possession" does not mean a person is not responsible for his own sin. His responsibility rests with the factors that led to his condition.

Possession can happen willingly. A person may desire to be taken over by spirit powers in order to conduct séances, pronounce curses, become a witch, or secure some other supernatural power. Possession can also occur unwillingly. An individual does not ask to be possessed, but it happens through sinful thoughts, actions, or contact with occult possession. Demonic powers operating in parents and the sins of the parents can affect the next generation.

Such situations can cause demonic obsession. This is a condition where one becomes obsessed by an interest in or a preoccupation with demons. It is an unusual attraction to the occult, demons, and Satan which controls interests and pursuits in a dictating manner. This obsession can eventually lead to possession by demonic spirits.

Many people ask me if a believer in Christ can be possessed by any form of demonic spirits. A true Christian cannot be possessed by a demon because the Holy Spirit cannot inhabit the same temple as an evil spirit. When you belong to God and are filled with the Holy Spirit, you cannot belong to Satan and be filled with his spirits at the same time. The Holy Ghost will not abide in the same "temple" with Satan. But this does not mean you cannot be affected by demonic powers. It is these powers against which we wrestle. Satan uses demonic powers to attack believers from the outside through oppression. But he cannot possess the true believer. To "possess" indicates inside occupation. To "oppress" or bind indicates control from the outside. The activities of believers can be satanically directed if they allow demonic powers to oppress them. Such oppression or binding by evil powers permits Satan to use them for evil purposes. This is what happened when Peter, a disciple of Jesus, was used by Satan to try to divert Jesus from suffering for the sins of all mankind. When Jesus described the suffering He was about to go through, "Peter took Him aside and began to rebuke Him, saying, 'Far be it from You, Lord; this shall not happen to You!'" (Matthew 16:22). Then Jesus "turned and said to Peter, 'Get behind Me, Satan! You are an offense to Me, for you are not mindful of the things of god, but the things of men'" (Matthew 16:23).

Jesus did not mean Peter was actually Satan. He recognized that at that moment, Peter had allowed Satan to operate through him. He was not demon-possessed, but he was allowing satanic spirits to influence him. When a person is born again, his name is written in a special book in Heaven called the book of life. Only those whose names are in this book will be residents of Heaven for eternity. It is also possible to have your name written in the book of life, but later blotted out because you turned back to sinful living.

If you continue in known, unconfessed sin, there is a point at which you can cease to be a Christian. The Apostle Paul expressed his own concern that he not be "cast away" after preaching to others. Paul realized that sin, especially continuous, unconfessed sins of the flesh, could result in the loss of his own soul even though he had preached to others. By continuing to live in sin, you will eventually end up in a backslidden condition. This means you will no longer be a true follower of Jesus Christ. If you continue in known, unconfessed sin, no one can tell you at what point you ceased to become a follower of Jesus and again become part of Satan's kingdom. It is God that determines that point. But when it occurs, you are opening yourself up to greater attacks of the enemy, including the possibility of demon possession. This is why it is important when you sin to immediately confess your sin and turn from unrighteousness. Jesus is called the Word of God in many places in scripture. If the Word of God does not dwell in you, then Jesus does not dwell in you.

*Can demonic spirits gain control over my life?* Yes, demonic spirits can gain control over your life, and it can be done in several ways, firstly, through generations or generational curses. Demons may oppress or possess a person because of previous possession or oppression of the parents. This accounts for demonic influence over children as seen in the following scriptures: "You shall not bow down to them nor serve them. For I, the Lord your God, am a jealous God, visiting the iniquity of the fathers upon the children to the third and fourth generations of those who hate Me" (Exodus 20:5).

"Keeping mercy for thousands, forgiving iniquity and transgression and sin, by no means clearing the guilty, visiting the iniquity of the fathers upon the children and the children's children to the third and the fourth generation" (Exodus 34:7).

"You shall not bow down to them nor serve them. For I, the Lord your God, am a jealous God, visiting the iniquity of the fathers upon the children to the third and fourth generations of those who hate Me" (Deuteronomy 5:9).

Secondly, Satan gains control over you through your mind. The mind is one of Satan's major battlefields. If Satan can control your thoughts, he will eventually control your actions. Lack of mental control eventually results in the inability to use your will. This leads to sinful actions. Continuing in sinful thoughts and actions can move from oppression to possession, and finally to a reprobate mind as the one described in Romans 1:28: "And even as they did not like to retain God in their knowledge, God gave them over to a debased mind, to do those things which are not fitting." This is a mind totally controlled by evil thoughts. Demons also gain access through mind-altering drugs, which increase the demon's access to your mind and reduce your ability to resist demons. "Brainwashing" or "mind control" teaching also provides an entrance point for demons.

Thirdly, Satan can gain control over you through sinful actions. Sinful thoughts are soon fulfilled by sinful actions. For example, the thought of adultery is fulfilled in the actual act of adultery. Sin is rebellion, and rebellious thoughts and actions provide an entry point for demonic activity. When a believer continues in sinful thoughts or actions, he or she "gives place" to the devil. The enemy is given more spiritual room for his operation. Sins of involvement with occult practices, including objects, literature, and séances are dangerous acts which attract demonic powers. A non-Christian who lives in sin is open not only to oppression of demonic powers, but also possession. As I mentioned before, there is no neutral ground in the spiritual realm. You are either on the side of good or evil. You belong either to God or Satan. If you belong to Satan and have not experienced the new birth in Jesus Christ, then you are his to use, oppress, or possess as he wills.

Fourthly, Satan can gain control over you through desire. Some people desire and request Satan so that they can be under the control of demonic powers. They do this for purposes of having supernatural power or performing supernatural acts. He can also gain control over you through an empty "house." Demons consider the body of the person they inhabit as their house. In Matthew 12:44, the Bible says, "Then he says, 'I will return to my house from which I came.' And when he comes, he finds it empty, swept, and put in order." When a person who has been delivered from demonic powers does not fill his spiritual house with the new birth experience and the infilling of the Holy Spirit, reentry may occur.

Lastly, Satan can gain control over you through permission. Sometimes, God grants permission for activities of demonic powers to accomplish special purposes. This can be allowed as a trial for believers as in the case of Job. It can also be judgment for sin as in the case of King Saul.

**Are you wondering how you can be ministered to if you are affected by demonic spirits?** Once you recognize that a demonic spirit is tormenting you or a family member, you must acknowledge that you or that person needs deliverance. Then, find a Christian minister or believer who has a strong prayer life and believes in the teachings of Jesus Christ and in the casting out of demons and seek your deliverance from that person. The best place to experience the power of God in deliverance is by attending a deliverance church service or deliverance crusade. I have personally seen thousands of people delivered in my miracle and deliverance crusades on a weekly basis.

Dealing with demonic powers is not something to be done by pastors or ministers only; any Bible-believing and -praying Christian can cast demonic spirits out. Jesus said all believers would have the ability to overcome demonic powers. Jesus has given His followers the ability to deal with demonic powers. He first delegated such power to the disciples, and then He delegated this same power to all believers.

There is no biblical basis for believing God intended this important ministry to be restricted to a particular group of people. A layman named Philip was used by God to cast out evil spirits in Samaria. "Therefore, those who were scattered went everywhere preaching the word. Then Philip went down to the city of Samaria and preached Christ to them. And the multitudes with one accord heeded the things spoken by Philip, hearing and seeing the miracles which he did. For unclean spirits, crying with a loud voice came out of many who were possessed; and many who were paralyzed and lame were healed. And there was great joy in that city" (Acts 8:4-8).

But this does not mean believers should rush into encounters with demonic powers without proper preparation, as the sons of Sceva discovered. "Also there were seven sons of Sceva, a Jewish chief priest, who did so. And the evil spirit answered and said, 'Jesus, I know, and Paul I know; but who are you?' Then the man in whom the evil spirit was leaped on them, overpowered them, and prevailed against them, so that they fled out of that house naked and wounded" (Acts 19:14-16). It is also important that believers do not become overly demon-conscious. We are not called to major in demons. There is no spiritual gift of "casting out demons." However, you should not be fearful of demonic powers. When confronted with those affected by demons, you should have the power to deliver them from bondage and bring them to God.

The teaching and ministry of Jesus demonstrated that demonic spirits are a real force of evil. What Jesus taught about demons and how He dealt with them provides valuable information about the strategies of Satan. Jesus accepted the fact that Satan is the ruler of a host of demons. He taught on the reality and power of demons. He said that the casting out of demonic powers was one of the signs that the Kingdom of God had come. The following scriptures provide a summary of what Jesus taught regarding demons:

> Then one was brought to Him who was demon-possessed, blind and mute; and He healed him so that the blind and mute man both

spoke and saw. And all the multitudes were amazed and said, "Could this be the Son of David?" Now when the Pharisees heard it, they said, "This fellow does not cast out demons except by Beelzebub, the ruler of the demons." But Jesus knew their thoughts, and said to them: "Every kingdom divided against itself is brought to desolation, and every city or house divided against itself will not stand. If Satan casts out Satan, he is divided against himself. How then will his kingdom stand? And if I cast out demons by Beelzebub, by whom do your sons cast them out? Therefore, they shall be your judges. But if I cast out demons by the Spirit of God, surely the kingdom of God has come upon you. Or how can one enter a strong man's house and plunder his goods, unless he first binds the strong man? And then he will plunder his house. He who is not with Me is against Me, and he who does not gather with Me scatters abroad (Matthew 12:22-30).

And the scribes who came down from Jerusalem said, "He has Beelzebub," and, "By the ruler of the demons He casts out demons." So He called them to Himself and said to them in parables: "How can Satan cast out Satan? If a kingdom is divided against itself, that kingdom cannot stand. And if a house is divided against itself, that house cannot stand. And if Satan has risen up against himself, and is divided, he cannot stand, but has an end. No one can enter a strong man's house and plunder his goods, unless he first binds the strong man. And then he will plunder his house (Mark 3:22-27).

And He was casting out a demon, and it was mute. So it was, when the demon had gone out, that the mute spoke; and the multitudes marveled. But some of them said, "He casts out demons by Beelzebub, the ruler of the demons." Others, testing Him, sought from Him a sign from heaven. But He, knowing their thoughts, said to them: "Every kingdom divided against itself is brought to desolation, and a house divided against a house falls. If Satan also is divided against himself, how will his kingdom stand? Because you say I cast out demons by Beelzebub. And if I cast out demons by Beelzebub, by whom do your sons cast them out? Therefore, they will be your judges. But if I cast out demons with the finger of God, surely the kingdom of God has come upon you. When a strong man, fully armed, guards his own palace, his goods are in peace. But when a stronger than he comes upon him and overcomes him, he takes from him all his armor in which he trusted, and divides his spoils. He who is not with Me is against Me, and he who does not gather with Me scatters (Luke 11:14-23).

A large portion of Jesus' ministry dealt with demons. The example that Jesus set and the authority of His name provides the scriptural basis for dealing with demonic powers. Jesus ministered to "all" who came with demonic problems.

To discern when demonic spirits attack, it is important to be able to recognize their presence, tactics, and operation in your life. The Holy Spirit has provided a special spiritual gift for this purpose. This gift is called "discerning of spirits" in 1 Corinthians 12:10 "to another the working of miracles, to another prophecy, to another discerning of spirits, to another different kinds of tongues, to another the interpretation of tongues." Discern means "to discover, evaluate, and make a distinction between." The gift of discerning of spirits enables you to discern the spirits operating within you or others. It permits you to discover, evaluate, and identify evil spirits. It prevents deception by seducing or lying spirits. With this gift you can recognize the evil tactics and motives of demonic powers. For example, some deafness and dumbness according to God's word is caused by demonic spirits. Other deaf and dumb cases may be the result of an accident or illness. Discernment would allow you to determine the cause of the condition as well as a remedy.

Not all Christians have this special spiritual gift of discerning of spirits. If a believer does not have this gift, there are signs of demonic presence which can be observed. Take for instance, when the Syrophoenician woman came to Jesus with an appeal for him to cast out an unclean spirit from her daughter. "And behold, a woman of

Canaan came from that region and cried out to Him, saying, 'Have mercy on me, O Lord, Son of David! My daughter is severely demon-possessed'" (Matthew 15:22). How did she know this? She knew it by the symptoms. Detection is simply observing what demonic spirits do to a person.

What are the symptoms of demonic activities? Demonic obsession is recognized by an uncontrollable and unusual preoccupation with demons, Satan, or the occult. Such a person may dabble in occult practices, constantly crediting everything to Satan or demons, or be preoccupied with the study of demons and Satan. Other symptoms of demonic activity include feelings of continual sickness and doctors being unable to identify what is wrong with you. You may feel movements in your body, be tormented by voices in your ears, or through dreams and visions or feel the presence of unseen things. You may even be sexually harassed in your sleep, and experience emptiness and tiredness. In other cases, you may be unable to accomplish your daily chores, experience sleepless nights, and uncontrollable behavior.

Demonic oppression can be recognized by the following signs:

A physical binding: The "daughter of Abraham" who Jesus relieved of a spirit of infirmity was bound physically.

> Now He was teaching in one of the synagogues on the Sabbath. And behold, there was a woman who had a spirit of infirmity eighteen years, and was bent over and could in no way raise herself up. But when Jesus saw her, He called her to Him and said to her, "Woman, you are loosed from your infirmity." And He laid His hands on her, and immediately she was made straight, and glorified God. But the ruler of the synagogue answered with indignation, because Jesus had healed on the Sabbath; and he said to the crowd, "There are six days on which men ought to work; therefore, come and be healed on them, and not on the Sabbath day." The Lord then answered him and said, "Hypocrite! Does not each one of you on the Sabbath loose his ox or donkey from the stall, and lead *it*

away to water it? So ought not this woman, being a daughter of Abraham, whom Satan has bound—think of it—for eighteen years, be loosed from this bond on the Sabbath?" And when He said these things, all His adversaries were put to shame; and all the multitude rejoiced for all the glorious things that were done by Him (Luke 13:10-17).

Chronic sickness may be demonic oppression. All illnesses are not caused by demonic powers. Some illnesses are caused by a violation of natural laws, such as not eating well or drinking contaminated water. Other illnesses may be attributed to chastisement. One king in the Bible who did not give glory to God was stricken with intestinal worms and died.

Mental oppression consists of disturbances in the mind or thought life such as mental torment, confusion, doubt, loss of memory, restlessness, inability to reason or listen to others, abnormal talkativeness or reservedness. All mental problems are not caused by Satan. Discouragement, depression, and disorientation can be caused by allergies to certain foods or a wrong chemical imbalance in the brain. God is able to heal mental problems and illnesses that are not caused by demonic powers as well as bring deliverance in cases caused by demons. However, be careful not to classify all illnesses or mental problems with demonic spirits. Sometimes, a simple change in diet or lifestyle will eliminate a physical problem. Other mental disturbances include emotional problems which persist or recur such as resentment, hatred, anger, fear, rejection, self-pity, jealousy, depression, worry, insecurity, and inferiority. Additionally, there are spiritual problems with extreme difficulties in overcoming sin, including sinful habits, rejection of spiritual solutions to problems or any type of doctrinal error or deception, including bondage to objects and literature of cults. Demons can create difficult circumstances which are oppressive. Such circumstances usually involve confusion and can immediately be identified as demonic because God is not the author of confusion. "For God is not the author of confusion but of peace, as in all the churches of the saints" (1 Corinthians 14:33).

How to recognize or discern when someone is demon-possessed? You can recognize when someone is demon-possessed through their behavior. For example, you can recognize them by the following signs:

- Indwelling of an unclean spirit: This is demonstrated by basic moral uncleanness and filthiness. It might include the desire to go without clothing. "And when He had come out of the boat, immediately there met Him out of the tombs a man with an unclean spirit" (Mark 5:2). "And when He stepped out on the land, there met Him a certain man from the city who had demons for a long time. And he wore no clothes, nor did he live in a house but in the tombs" (Luke 8:27).

- Unusual physical strength: A person shows strength beyond normal capabilities. "Who had his dwelling among the tombs; and no one could bind him, not even with chains" (Mark 5:3). "For He had commanded the unclean spirit to come out of the man. For it had often seized him, and he was kept under guard, bound with chains and shackles; and he broke the bonds and was driven by the demon into the wilderness" (Luke 8:29).

- Fits of rage: These fits may be accompanied by foaming at the mouth.

And when He came to the disciples, He saw a great multitude around them, and scribes disputing with them. Immediately, when they saw Him, all the people were greatly amazed, and running to Him, greeted Him. And He asked the scribes, "What are you discussing with them?" Then one of the crowd answered and said, "Teacher, I brought You my son, who has a mute spirit. And wherever it seizes him, it throws him down; he foams at the mouth, gnashes his teeth, and becomes rigid. So I spoke to Your disciples, that they should cast it out, but they could not." He answered him and said, "O faithless generation, how long shall I be with you? How long shall I bear with you? Bring him to Me." Then they brought him to Him. And when he saw Him, immediately the spirit convulsed him, and he fell on the ground and wallowed, foaming at the mouth. So He asked his father, "How long has this been happening to him?" And he said, ">From childhood. And often he has thrown him both into the fire and into the water to destroy him. But if You can do anything, have compassion on us and help us." Jesus said to him, "If you can believe, all things are possible to him who believes." Immediately, the father of the child cried out and said with tears, "Lord, I believe; help my unbelief!" When Jesus saw that the people came running together, He rebuked the unclean spirit, saying to it: "Deaf and dumb spirit, I command you, come out of him and enter him no more!" Then the spirit cried out, convulsed him greatly, and came out of him. And he became as one dead, so that many said, "He is dead." But Jesus took him by the hand and lifted him up, and he arose. And when He had come into the house, His disciples asked Him privately, "Why could we not cast it out?" So He said to them, "This kind can come out by nothing but prayer and fasting" (Mark 9:14-29).

Then they sailed to the country of the Gadarenes, which is opposite Galilee. And when He stepped out on the land, there met Him a certain man from the city who had demons for a long time. And he wore no clothes, nor did he live in a house but in the tombs. When he saw Jesus, he cried out, fell down before Him, and with a loud voice said, "What have I to do with You, Jesus, Son of the Most High God? I beg You, do not torment me!" For He had commanded the unclean spirit to come out of the man. For it had often seized him, and he was kept under guard, bound with chains and shackles; and he broke the bonds and was driven by the demon into the wilderness. Jesus asked him, saying, "What is your name?" And he said, "Legion," because many demons had entered him. And they begged Him that He would not command them to go out into the abyss. Now a herd of many swine was feeding there on the mountain. So they begged Him that He would permit them to enter them. And He permitted them. Then the demons went out of the man and entered the swine, and the herd ran violently down the steep place into the lake and drowned. When those who fed *them* saw what had happened, they fled and told *it* in the city and in the country. Then they went out to see what had happened, and came to Jesus, and found the man from whom the demons had departed, sitting at the feet of Jesus, clothed and in his right mind. And they were afraid. They also who had seen *it* told them by what means he who had been demon-possessed was healed. Then the whole multitude of the surrounding region of the Gadarenes asked Him to depart from them, for they were seized with great fear. And He got into the boat and returned. Now the man from whom the demons had departed begged Him that he might be with Him. But Jesus sent him away, saying, "Return to your own house, and tell what great things God has done for you." And he went his way and proclaimed throughout the whole city what great things Jesus had done for him (Luke 8:26-39).

- Resistance to spiritual things: In the accounts in Mark 1:21-28 and Mark 6:7, the demons knew Jesus immediately and asked Him to leave them alone. Fear of the name of Jesus, prayer, and the word and blasphemy of that which is spiritual are all symptoms of demon possession. Excessive blasphemy may be noted or contorted physical features and abrupt behavior changes when spiritual things are mentioned.

  Then they went into Capernaum, and immediately on the Sabbath He entered the synagogue and taught. And they were astonished at His teaching, for He taught them as one having authority, and not as the scribes. Now there was a man in their synagogue with an unclean spirit. And he cried out, saying, "Let *us* alone! What have we to do with You, Jesus of Nazareth? Did You come to destroy us? I know who You are—the Holy One of God!" But Jesus rebuked him, saying, "Be quiet, and come out of him!" And when the unclean spirit had convulsed him and cried out with a loud voice, he came out of him. Then they were all amazed, so that they questioned among themselves, saying, "What is this? What new doctrine *is* this? For with authority He commands even the unclean spirits, and they obey Him." And immediately His fame spread throughout the region around Galilee (Mark 1:21-28).

"And He called the twelve to Himself, and began to send them out two *by* two, and gave them power over unclean spirits" (Mark 6:7).

- Changes in personality and/or voice: A person who is normally shy may become aggressive or violent. Actions as well as appearance may be affected. Moral character and intelligence may change. Voice may be altered.

    Then He asked him, "What is your name?" And he answered, saying, "My name is Legion; for we are many" (Mark 5:9).

- Accompanying physical afflictions: In cases of demon possession, these appear most commonly to be afflictions of the mental and nervous system.

    "And when the demon was cast out, the mute spoke. And the multitudes marveled, saying, 'It was never seen like this in Israel!'" (Matthew 9:33)

    "Then one was brought to Him who was demon-possessed, blind and mute; and He healed him so that the blind and mute man both spoke and saw" (Matthew 12:22).

    "Because he had often been bound with shackles and chains. And the chains had been pulled apart by him, and the shackles broken in pieces; neither could anyone tame him" (Mark 5:4-5).

They can also include a general "pining" or wasting away physically.

And when He came to the disciples, He saw a great multitude around them, and scribes disputing with them. Immediately, when they saw Him, all the people were greatly amazed, and running to Him, greeted Him. And He asked the scribes, "What are you discussing with them?" Then one of the crowd answered and said, "Teacher, I brought You my son, who has a mute spirit. And wherever it seizes him, it throws him down; he foams at the mouth, gnashes his teeth, and becomes rigid. So I spoke to Your disciples, that they should cast it out, but they could not." He answered him and said, "O faithless generation, how long shall I be with you? How long shall I bear with you? Bring him to me." Then they brought him to Him. And when he saw Him, immediately the spirit convulsed him, and he fell on the ground and wallowed, foaming at the mouth. So He asked his father, "How long has this been happening to him?" And he said, ">from childhood. And often he has thrown him both into the fire and into the water to destroy him. But if You can do anything, have compassion on us and help us." Jesus said to him, "If you can believe, all things *are* possible to him who believes." Immediately, the father of the child cried out and said with tears, "Lord, I believe; help my unbelief!" When Jesus saw that the people came running together, He rebuked the unclean spirit, saying to it: "Deaf and dumb spirit, I command you, come out of him and enter him no more!" Then *the spirit* cried out, convulsed him greatly, and came out of him. And he became as one dead, so that many said, "He is dead." But Jesus took him by the hand and lifted him up, and he arose. And when He had come into the house, His disciples asked Him privately, "Why could we not cast it out?" So He said to them, "This kind can come out by nothing but prayer and fasting" (Mark 9:14-29).

- Self-inflicted physical injury: In Matthew 17:14-21, there is the story of a man's son who would cast himself in the fire. In Luke 8:26-39, this demon-possessed man cut himself with stones to inflict physical injury.

And when they had come to the multitude, a man came to Him, kneeling down to Him and saying, "Lord, have mercy on my son, for he is an epileptic and suffers severely; for he often falls into the fire and often into the water. So I brought him to

Your disciples, but they could not cure him." Then Jesus answered and said, "O faithless and perverse generation, how long shall I be with you? How long shall I bear with you? Bring him here to Me." And Jesus rebuked the demon, and it came out of him; and the child was cured from that very hour. Then the disciples came to Jesus privately and said, "Why could we not cast it out?" So Jesus said to them, "Because of your unbelief; for assuredly, I say to you, if you have faith as a mustard seed, you will say to this mountain, 'Move from here to there,' and it will move; and nothing will be impossible for you. However, this kind does not go out except by prayer and fasting" (Matthew 17:14-21).

Then they sailed to the country of the Gadarenes, which is opposite Galilee. And when He stepped out on the land, there met Him a certain man from the city who had demons for a long time. And he wore no clothes, nor did he live in a house but in the tombs. When he saw Jesus, he cried out, fell down before Him, and with a loud voice said, "What have I to do with You, Jesus, Son of the Most High God? I beg You, do not torment me!" For He had commanded the unclean spirit to come out of the man. For it had often seized him, and he was kept under guard, bound with chains and shackles; and he broke the bonds and was driven by the demon into the wilderness. Jesus asked him, saying, "What is your name?" And he said, "Legion," because many demons had entered him. And they begged Him that He would not command them to go out into the abyss. Now a herd of many swine was feeding there on the mountain. So they begged Him that He would permit them to enter them. And He permitted them. Then the demons went out of the man and entered the swine, and the herd ran violently down the steep place into the lake and drowned. When those who fed *them* saw what had happened, they fled and told *it* in the city and in the country. Then they went out to see what had happened, and came to Jesus, and found the man from whom the demons had departed, sitting at the feet of Jesus, clothed and in his right mind. And they were afraid. They also who had seen *it* told them by what means he who had been demon-possessed was healed. Then the whole multitude of the surrounding region of the Gadarenes asked Him to depart from them, for they were seized with great fear. And He got into the boat and returned. Now the man from whom the demons had departed begged Him that he might be with Him. But Jesus sent him away, saying, "Return to your own house, and tell what great things God has done for you." And he went his way and proclaimed throughout the whole city what great things Jesus had done for him (Luke 8:26-39).

- Terrible anguish: Luke 8:28 relates that this man went about crying because of the terrible inner torments caused by his possession. When he saw Jesus, he cried out, fell down before Him, and with a loud voice said, "What have I to do with You, Jesus, Son of the Most High God? I beg You, do not torment me!"

- Incapacity for normal living: This man could not live in society but lived in the tombs of the cemetery. "And when He stepped out on the land, there met Him a certain man from the city who had demons for a long time. And he wore no clothes, nor did he live in a house but in the tombs" (Luke 8:27).

- Through unscriptural methods, the ability to foretell the future or discover that which is unknown: The woman in Acts 16:16 is said to be "possessed" by a spirit of divination. "Now it happened, as we went to prayer, that a certain slave girl possessed with a spirit of divination met us, who brought her masters much profit by fortune-telling."

- Obsessive immorality such as involvement with pornography, adultery, fornication, masturbation, homosexuality, and other sex sins. Strong compulsions toward eating disorders, suicide, self-mutilation, maiming, and murder.

- Addiction to drugs or alcohol.

- Trances, visions, and meditation which are not focused on or from the one true God.

- Bondage to emotions such as fear, anxiety, depression, hatred, rage, jealousy, backbiting, envy, pride, bitterness, negativism, and criticism.

There are some scriptural strategies on how you can be delivered from demonic spirits. You must prepare yourself for deliverance. The Bible says, faith comes by hearing the Word of God, the specific or "Rhema" Word. Begin to build faith in your heart by reading the Bible through with a new attitude, and acknowledge that you are a sinner and Jesus Christ died for you and only he can wash you and cleanse you and deliver you from sin and every demonic force.

- Whatever Jesus told His followers to do, you begin to do.

- Whatever He said He would do, expect Him to do it.

- If He said you can deliver those afflicted by Satan, then expect to see them delivered.

- If He said to cast out devils, then do it in His name and expect them to obey you. Disregard all the teachings of man and personal experiences you have had. Accept that the Bible means exactly what it says. Accept it as true, and act accordingly.

# Chapter Five:
# Understanding Deliverance

> "Rescue me and deliver me from the hand of foreigners,
> whose mouth speaks lying words, and whose right hand
> is a right hand of falsehood."
> Psalm 144:11

Preparing yourself to receive and maintain your deliverance is a very important process. I will walk you through some of the basic steps. You must understand that while deliverance can be a one-time event, it can also be a process. If you do not receive your freedom the first time you seek deliverance, do not be discouraged. Keep pressing forward to receive what Jesus purchased for you with His blood on the cross. Sometimes, it takes more time to dig out all the junk from your soul. You may have one session or several sessions of deliverance, ranging from a few minutes to several hours, depending on the bondage that is being addressed in your life.

Sometimes, it may even take more than one person or intercessor to pray for your deliverance as the Bible says in Matthew 17:21: "However, this kind does not go out except by prayer and fasting." When it comes to your deliverance, you should envision your broken life being restored to the one that God has destined for you. It is easy to think of your deliverance as a quick-fix—simply casting out demons and releasing yourself from bondage. But deliverance involves more than driving out demons. There are usually strongholds to be torn down. Since strongholds are incorrect thinking patterns, you must renew your mind through the Word of God... I cannot stress enough how important it is to pursue an intimate relationship with the Lord once you have been delivered. If you neglect your relationship with God, the enemy would be more than happy to cause you to lose your newfound freedom.

The purpose of your deliverance is to receive freedom from any hindrances that would keep you from having a relationship with God and walking in the fullness of God's plan for your life. The following four elements will provide you with a deeper understanding of what you will have to go through to experience deliverance:

- Legal grounds are things in a person's life which are giving or have given a demon the right to enter or remain in that person. Unconfessed sins, ungodly soul ties, unforgiveness, and holding cursed possessions such as occult rings can give demons a right to inhabit and torment you. These legal grounds are removed through repentance, renunciation, and forgiveness.

- Strongholds are incorrect thinking patterns in your mind. If you think that God is angry with you, then you will feel like He is angry with you when nothing could be further from the truth. If you think you are worthless, then you will feel worthless. Strongholds are torn down as you meditate on deliverance scriptures such as 2 Timothy 4:18, which re-program your mind to think differently. "And the Lord will deliver me from every evil work and preserve me for His heavenly kingdom. To Him be glory forever and ever. Amen!" If God sees you as a precious child of His and you begin to realize and believe that, then it will change the way you see yourself.

- Inner healing is often required when ministering to someone who has been abused, raped, or exposed to a traumatic experience. It is a working of the Holy Spirit which is received as a person releases the inner hurt and pain from past experiences and allows the Holy Spirit to come in and heal those wounds. Forgiveness often plays a part in this releasing process and it is done by faith (even if you do not feel like you could ever forgive someone for the damage that person did). Oftentimes, you must forgive yourself to be released from self-destructive thinking patterns that have hindered your progress.

- Casting out demons must not be overlooked as it entails the process of expelling demons in Jesus' name from a demon-possessed person. Even if you experience a degree of freedom after tearing down strongholds and breaking up legal grounds, demons may still be present and need to be cast out.

During deliverance, there are times that you may manifest a demon, while on other occasions it may appear as if nothing is happening when it is being expelled. Mild manifestations often involve coughing, spitting up phlegm, burping, deep yawning or sighing, pressure or pain in areas of your body, shaking and screaming. If you begin experiencing these manifestations, do not resist. Allow the demons to manifest and come forth. Stronger manifestations are usually found in cases where a person is being delivered from severe oppression, deliverance from occult involvement or Satanism. Oftentimes, you are unconscious when these spirits manifest. Such spirits trigger demonic convulsions and body levitations and cause you to struggle physically with those delivering you. In cases where you may enter a deep sleep, the person conducting your deliverance should not interrupt your rest. This is recommended to allow the demon to emerge from within you, so that you can confront it. Feelings or emotions will often rise up as spirits are confronted. For example, if we are dealing with a spirit of grief, the person may experience deep levels of grief as the spirit is manifesting and being driven out.

Demons may speak through you, at times, to the person who is helping you. Sometimes, they will simply take control of your mouth and speak. You may or may not be aware of this when it happens, but do not try to prevent it. If you hear yourself spewing out curses and foul language toward the person helping you, do not be ashamed as this is all part of the process.

Sometimes, spirits can be stubborn and require persistence to drive them out. If the person helping you repeatedly confronts the same spirit, do not be alarmed. Many times the person conducting the deliverance has to dedicate more time to getting the demon to emerge from within you so that it can be destroyed. Demons can resist your authority; therefore, they require persistent pressure before they cooperate. Through the entire process of your deliverance, the enemy may bombard you with doubt and fear and make you feel like you will never be set free. I advise you to fight those feelings as much as you can. Saying to yourself, "I will never be set free" doubts the work that God is trying to do for you and wages war against your faith. Instead you can say, "I resist those feelings and I believe in the work that Jesus Christ is doing in my life."

It is important to be brave when battling your demons. God is much more powerful, and His angels are here to assist you. You may encounter some strong spirits that will resist your authority. That is why you must be persistent. Your freedom has been paid for by the precious Blood of Jesus Christ, and you must stand on that promise as you confront the spirits at hand.

When demons are manifesting or being driven out of you, it is usually best not to do much talking. Spirits often leave through your mouth and you can hold them back from coming out if you obstruct their passageway. If you feel something evil coming up your throat, do not stop its departure. Allow it to come forth. Hanging onto your bondage can literally keep you from being delivered. It is important to "let go" and allow the demons to be released. Trying to remove a spirit of fear, while your mind is wondering whether or not to be in agreement, is not an easy task. You must be persistent with your faith in Jesus Christ.

Throughout the deliverance process, the Holy Spirit may bring to your remembrance a past sin or situation that may have opened the door to demons. Confess those sins and ask for forgiveness so that it will remove any legal grounds to those spirits. If you feel the Holy Spirit sharing anything with you during your deliverance, do not hesitate to share it with the person that is delivering. Most times you will experience things that the person who is helping you cannot perceive. For example, physical pain in an area of your body indicates a spirit manifesting. If the person who is helping you knows where it is, he may place a Bible over that area of your body and confront the spirit. If you feel any discomfort, pain or pressure in your body, confusion, headache, racing or irrational emotions rising up in your mind, then you should inform that person of what is happening. If you are released from a spirit or sense that something has left your body, start worshiping God.

If you experience any feelings of anger, hate, rage, rebellion or the desire to run out of the room where you are being delivered, I recommend that you tell the person who is helping you about what is happening. Always keep that person informed regarding what is going on inside of you, unless he is in the midst of casting it out and you feel it coming out of your mouth. As I mentioned before, it is important that you avoid speaking or obstructing your airways as the demons are being expelled.

You are always the best person to determine whether the spirit has left. Did you feel a release or relief as if something has left you? Inform the person delivering you of this occurrence. Sometimes, spirits can go into hiding to trick you into thinking they are gone, and other times there are additional spirits to be driven out. Normally, when you feel a release, it means that the spirits have departed.

# Chapter Six:
# The Armor of God

"Finally, my brethren, be strong in the Lord and in the power of His might. [11] Put on the whole armor of God that you may be able to stand against the wiles of the devil. [12] For we do not wrestle against flesh and blood, but against principalities, against powers, against the rulers of the darkness of this age, against spiritual *hosts* of wickedness in the heavenly *places.*"

*Ephesians 6:10-12*

Many people ask me, "Bishop Robin, can you teach me how to pray?" I am willing to teach anyone how to pray; however, my way may not work for you. The best way to learn how to pray is the way Jesus taught His disciples. You can follow this pattern through the scriptures below.

Let's take a close look at the model prayer. When the disciples came to Jesus, they said, "Teach us to pray," not "Teach us a prayer." Jesus responded to their request by using a method commonly employed by the Jewish rabbi. The rabbi often listed certain topics of truth, and under each category provided a complete outline. In this model prayer, Jesus used the same teaching pattern. He gave topics and instructed, "After this manner, therefore, pray."

**Our Father:** The words *Our Father* indicate nearness, but the words *in heaven* imply distance. Psalm 139 reveals, however, that God is everywhere.

*Robin Dinnanauth*

        O Lord, You have searched me and known me.

You know my sitting down and my rising up;
You understand my thought afar off.
You comprehend my path and my lying down,
And are acquainted with all my ways.
For there is not a word on my tongue,
But behold, O Lord, You know it altogether.
You have hedged me behind and before,
And laid Your hand upon me.
Such knowledge is too wonderful for me;
It is high, I cannot attain it.
Where can I go from Your Spirit?
Or where can I flee from Your presence?
If I ascend into heaven, You are there;
If I make my bed in hell, behold, You are there.
If I take the wings of the morning,
And dwell in the uttermost parts of the sea,
Even there Your hand shall lead me,
And Your right hand shall hold me.
If I say, "Surely, the darkness shall fall on me,"
Even the night shall be light about me;
Indeed, the darkness shall not hide from You,
But the night shines as the day;
The darkness and the light are both alike to You.

For You formed my inward parts;
You covered me in my mother's womb.
I will praise You, for I am fearfully and wonderfully made;
Marvelous are Your works,
And that my soul knows very well.
My frame was not hidden from You,
When I was made in secret,
And skillfully wrought in the lowest parts of the earth.
Your eyes saw my substance, being yet unformed.
And in Your book they all were written,

The days fashioned for me,
When as yet there were none of them.
How precious also are Your thoughts to me, O God!
How great is the sum of them!
If I should count them, they would be more in number than the sand;
When I awake, I am still with You.
Oh, that You would slay the wicked, O God!
Depart from me, therefore, you bloodthirsty men.
For they speak against You wickedly;
Your enemies take Your name in vain.
Do I not hate them, O Lord, who hates You?
And do I not loathe those who rise up against You?
I hate them with perfect hatred;
I count them my enemies.
Search me, O God, and know my heart;
Try me, and know my anxieties;
And see if there is any wicked way in me,
And lead me in the way everlasting (Psalms 139).

When you pray to our Father in heaven, it does not emphasize the distance between you and the Father, but it immediately brings you from the natural world to a powerful spiritual plane. It assures you that God has all the resources of the supernatural realm at His disposal which He uses to respond to the requests presented in the remainder of the model prayer. When you pray "our Father in heaven," you are immediately linked through Christ with a supernatural God who has unlimited supernatural resources that can be used in prayer.

**Hallowed Be Your Name:** When you become members of God's family, our heavenly Father's name is given to you, just as a child who is adopted in the natural world assumes the name of his new father. Our spiritual adoption gives us the right to call God "Father" and receive all the benefits associated with His name, because you are now an heir of your Father's kingdom. God's name is not just an identification label, but it is an expression of His nature and identity. When you say "hallowed be Your name," you proclaim the person, power, and authority of God. The following list identifies the seven compound names of God and their meanings:

| Name | Meaning | Reference |
| --- | --- | --- |
| Jehovah-Tsidkenu | Jehovah our righteousness | Jeremiah 23:6 |
| Jehovah-M'kaddesh | Jehovah who sanctifies | Exodus 31:13 |
| Jehovah-Shalom | Jehovah is peace | Judges 6:24 |
| Jehovah-Shammah | Jehovah is there | Ezekiel 48:35 |
| Jehovah-Rophe | Jehovah heals | Exodus 15:26 |
| Jehovah-Jireh | Jehovah my provider | Genesis 22:14 |
| Jehovah-Nissi | Jehovah my banner | Exodus 17:15 |
| Jehovah-Rohi | Jehovah my shepherd | Psalm 23:1 |

When you pray for others, you can use these names to intercede for God to work in their lives. Here is an example: "I pray that you will be Jehovah-Shalom to my wife. I pray that you will be her Jehovah-Jireh, providing her every need this day. Jehovah-Nissi, I pray that your banner will reign over her life. I pray that as Jehovah-M'kaddesh, you will sanctify her this day."

**Your Kingdom Come:** In Greek, Hebrew, and Aramaic, the term *kingdom of God* refers to the kingship, sovereignty, reign, or ruling activity of God. It is the expression of God's nature in action. God's realm of operation can be viewed in terms of its inclusive universal organization as the kingdom of God; its local visible organization as the church through which the kingdom is extended; and individuals of which the kingdom is composed, that is, all true believers born into this kingdom.

Sometime in the future, the kingdom of God will be established in visible form. We do not know the exact timing of this as the Bible says in Acts 1:7: "And He said to them, 'It is not for you to know times or seasons which the Father has put in His own authority.'" So according to the Word of God, it is certain that all the kingdoms of the world will become the property of God, the evil kingdom of Satan will be defeated, and our King will reign forever. Revelation 11:15 says, "Then the seventh angel sounded: And there were loud voices in heaven, saying, 'The kingdoms of this world have become the kingdoms of our Lord and of His Christ, and He shall reign forever and ever!'"

The centrality of the kingdom message is clear in the New Testament. It is mentioned several times in Matthew, 16 times in Mark, and 38 times in Luke. Jesus began His earthly ministry by declaring the arrival of the kingdom. ">From that time Jesus began to preach and to say, 'Repent, for the kingdom of heaven is at hand'" (Matthew 4:17). He ended His earthly ministry by speaking of things pertaining to the kingdom. "To whom He also presented Himself alive after His suffering by many infallible proofs, being seen by them during forty days and speaking of the things pertaining to the kingdom of God" (Acts 1:3). In between the beginning and ending of His earthly ministry, the emphasis was always on the kingdom. He was constantly declaring He must preach its message in other places. "But He said to them, 'I must preach the kingdom of God to the other cities also, because for this purpose I have been sent'" (Luke 4:43). Every parable of Jesus related to the kingdom, and His life patterned its principles.

Jesus indicated that we, as believers, were to give similar emphasis to the kingdom: "But seek first the kingdom of God and His righteousness, and all these things shall be added to you" (Matthew 6:33). This verse indicates where we should focus our praying, preaching, teaching, and living. It should all be targeted to the kingdom of God. If we seek first the kingdom, it assures the answer to the other petitions that follow in the model prayer.

Praying "Your kingdom come" is more than a prayer for the return of Jesus and the establishment of His kingdom in its final form. In fact, when we pray "Your kingdom come," we are actually declaring that our Father will reign in the lives of believers, unbelievers, and the entire earth. We are interceding that God will be acknowledged as King, and that life here on earth will be regulated by His commands. When we say "Your kingdom come," we are actually asking God to remove anything that is in rebellion against His kingdom such as words, attitudes, desires, and behavior in ourselves and others.

**Your Will Be Done on Earth as It Is in Heaven:** In general, the Bible refers to the will of God in three different senses.

1. In some passages, *the will of God* is another way of saying "the law of God." "As we have heard, so we have seen in the city of the Lord of hosts, in the city of our God: God will establish it forever" (Psalm 48:8).

2. *The will of God* is also used to designate anything that God expressly desires. This may be called God's "perfect will." "Who desires all men to be saved and to come to the knowledge of the truth" (1 Timothy 2:4).

3. Finally, *the will of God* may refer to what God permits or allows to happen. This may be called God's "permissive will." "And do not be conformed to this world, but be transformed by the renewing of your mind, that you may prove what *is* that good and acceptable and perfect will of God" (Romans 12:2).

The Bible's teaching about the will of God expresses more than mere doctrine; it intersects with your life as a believer on an everyday basis. You must learn what God's will is, and you must commit yourself to do His will. You must pray that God's will and purpose be fulfilled in your life according to His eternal plan. If this is your prayer and commitment, then you can rest assured that your present and future are in the protective care of your heavenly Father. You can determine God's will primarily through His Word, the Bible, and the Holy Spirit's leading in your heart.

**Give Us This Day Our Daily Bread:** In the model prayer, we seek first the kingdom when we declare "Your kingdom come" over every circumstance in our lives. We submit in righteousness to our heavenly Father's will, declaring, "Your will be done." Now we can pray with assurance, "Give us this day our daily bread," asking that our needs be met to enable us to fulfill His will and extend His kingdom.

"Give us" acknowledges that God is our source, not a denomination or a company paycheck. The Greek word translated "daily" in this model prayer occurs nowhere else in the Bible. It means "necessary or essential bread, sufficient for our sustenance and support." Its use in this context confirms that the model prayer Jesus taught is to be prayed each day. The prayer is for "bread," which indicates both spiritual and material sustenance. The word "us" denotes that we intercede for this daily bread of provision for others as well as ourselves.

**And Forgive Us Our Debts, as We Forgive Our Debtors:** We must learn to both receive and give forgiveness for personal offenses and injustices inflicted on us by others. Personal offenses occur when we offend ourselves and God through our own sin, and we deal with it by asking Him to forgive us when we say, "Forgive us our debts." The Bible declares, "If we say that we have no sin, we deceive ourselves, and the truth is not in us. If we confess our sins, He is faithful and just to forgive us our sins and to cleanse us from all unrighteousness" (1 John 1:8–9). When we confess our known sin, God forgives our unknown sin as well as what we have confessed, cleansing us from *all* unrighteousness.

The second area in which forgiveness must be manifested is in forgiving others of direct and indirect offenses. A direct offense occurs when we are offended by someone. Indirect offenses occur when someone hurts a friend or relative and we take up the offense. Jesus taught that we were to deal with such misdeeds by praying, "Forgive us our debts, as we forgive our debtors." The literal rendering of this verse in Greek is "as we forgive our debtors." Thus, the verse could read, "Forgive us our debts, as we have forgiven others." The idea is that before we ever seek forgiveness for our sins against God, we are to have already forgiven those who have sinned against us.

Jesus taught this principle in the parable of the unjust servant in Matthew 18:22–35.

> Jesus said to him, "I do not say to you, up to seven times, but up to seventy times seven. Therefore, the kingdom of heaven is like a certain king who wanted to settle accounts with his servants. And when he had begun to settle accounts, one was brought to him who owed him ten thousand talents. But as he was not able to pay, his master commanded that he be sold, with his wife and children and all that he had, and that payment be made. The servant therefore fell down before him, saying, 'Master, have patience with me, and I will pay you all.' Then the master of that servant was moved with compassion, released him, and forgave him the debt. "But that servant went out and found one of his fellow servants who owed him a hundred denarii; and he laid hands on him and took him by the throat, saying, 'Pay me what you owe!' So his fellow servant fell down at his feet[d] and begged him, saying, 'Have patience with me, and I will pay you all.' And he would not, but went and threw him into prison till he should pay the debt. So when his fellow servants saw what had been done, they were very grieved, and came and told their master all that had been done. Then his master, after he had called him, said to him, 'You wicked servant! I forgave you all that debt because you begged me. Should you not also have had compassion on your fellow servant, just as I had pity on you?' And his master was angry, and delivered him to the torturers until he should pay all that was due to him. "So My heavenly Father also will do to you if each of you, from his heart, does not forgive his brother his trespasses" (Matthew 18:22–35).

This story illustrates that God's forgiveness precedes human forgiveness. Human forgiveness is a reflection of God's forgiveness, and God's forgiveness becomes real for us only when we are willing to forgive one another. Jesus summarized these truths when He declared: "If you have anything against anyone, forgive him, that your Father in heaven may also forgive your trespasses. But if you do not forgive, neither will your Father in heaven forgive your trespasses" (Mark 11:25).

Satan causes offenses in your family, between friends, in your business relationships, and in your church. The Bible states that "offenses will come." "Woe to the world because of offenses! For offenses must come, but woe to that man by whom the offense comes!" (Matthew 18:7). How will you deal with these issues when they arise? Will you intercede about them in prayer or talk about them through gossip?

**And Do Not Lead Us into Temptation, But Deliver Us from the Evil One:** Jesus taught us to pray, "Do not lead us into temptation," but James indicates God does not tempt man: "Let no one say when he is tempted, 'I am tempted by God'; for God cannot be tempted by evil, nor does He Himself tempt anyone" (James 1:13). So who is the tempter to whom Jesus is referring? The Bible clearly reveals that this is the role of our enemy, Satan. "Now when the tempter came to Him, he said, 'If You are the Son of God, command that these stones become bread'" (Matthew 4:3). "For this reason, when I could no longer endure it, I sent to know your faith, lest by some means the tempter had tempted you, and our labor might be in vain" (1 Thessalonians 3:5).

The scriptures repeatedly warn us of temptations that come from the devil. "Then Jesus was led up by the Spirit into the wilderness to be tempted by the devil" (Matthew 4:1). "Do not deprive one another except with consent for a time, that you may give yourselves to fasting and prayer; and come together again so that Satan does not tempt you because of your lack of self-control" (1 Corinthians 7:5). The Bible explains that "But each one is tempted when he is drawn away by his own desires and enticed. When desire has conceived, it gives birth to sin; and sin, when it is full grown, brings forth death" (James 1:14–15). Satan is the tempter, but we are drawn into his snare when we allow our fleshly desires to entice us. Such desires birth sin, and sin results in death. Some of Satan's attacks arise from uncontrolled evil passions from within us, while other temptations come from outside through our senses of hearing, seeing, feeling, touching, or tasting. Whatever their source, the apostle Paul assures us, "No temptation has overtaken you except such as is common to man; but God is faithful, who will not allow you to be tempted beyond what you are able, but with the temptation will also make the way of escape, that you may be able to bear it" (1 Corinthians 10:13).

When we pray, "Do not lead us into temptation," we are asking God to preserve us from the enticement to sin. Even Jesus was not delivered from temptation, but was preserved in it. "For we do not have a High Priest who cannot sympathize with our weaknesses, but was in all points tempted as we are, yet without sin" (Hebrews 4:15). The apostle John assures us, "We know (absolutely) that any one born of God does not (deliberately and knowingly) practice committing sin, but the One Who was begotten of God carefully watches over and protects him—Christ's divine presence within him preserves him against the evil—and the wicked one does not lay hold (get a grip) on him or touch (him)" (1 John 5:18 AMP).

In Ephesians 6:10–18, the apostle Paul provides detailed information about the evil one and the spiritual armor that God provides for our defense. Paul emphatically declares we should be strong in the Lord and in the power of His might and stand boldly in the face of these evil forces.

> Finally, my brethren, be strong in the Lord and in the power of His might. Put on the whole armor of God that you may be able to stand against the wiles of the devil. For we do not wrestle against flesh and blood, but against principalities, against powers, against the rulers of the darkness of this age, against spiritual hosts of wickedness in the heavenly places. Therefore, take up the whole armor of God that you may be able to withstand in the evil day, and having done all, to stand. Stand therefore, having girded your waist with truth, having put on the breastplate of righteousness, and having shod your feet with the preparation of the gospel of peace; above all, taking the shield of faith with which you will be able to quench all the fiery darts of the wicked one. And take the helmet of salvation, and the sword of the Spirit, which is the word of God; praying always with all prayer and supplication in the

Spirit, being watchful to this end with all perseverance and supplication for all the saints (Ephesians 6:10-18).

He decrees that it is possible to stand against every wile (deceit, cunning, craftiness) of the devil. Paul admonishes that we should:

- War a good warfare: "This charge I commit to you, son Timothy, according to the prophecies previously made concerning you, that by them you may wage the good warfare" (1 Timothy 1:18).
- Fight an effective fight of faith: "Fight the good fight of faith, lay hold on eternal life, to which you were also called and have confessed the good confession in the presence of many witnesses" (1 Timothy 6:12)
- Battle intelligently with purpose: "Therefore, I run thus: not with uncertainty. Thus I fight: not as *one who* beats the air" (1 Corinthians 9:26).

Paul emphasizes that the battle is not a natural one, and that natural weapons are ineffective. Spiritual battles must be fought with spiritual weapons.

> Therefore, take up the whole armor of God that you may be able to withstand in the evil day, and having done all to stand. Stand therefore, having girded your waist with truth, having put on the breastplate of righteousness, and having shod your feet with the preparation of the gospel of peace; above all, taking the shield of faith with which you will be able to quench all the fiery darts of the wicked one. And take the helmet of salvation, and the sword of the Spirit, which is the word of God; praying always with all prayer and supplication in the Spirit, being watchful to this end with all perseverance and supplication for all the saints (Ephesians 6:13–18).

The purpose of the armor is to enable you to stand against the wiles of the enemy, Satan. Paul commands you to put on this spiritual armor, which means it is your responsibility to appropriate what God has provided. To "put on" means you take hold of something and apply it to yourself.

**For Yours Is the Kingdom and the Power and the Glory Forever:** The word *for* indicates the authority by which the model prayer has been prayed. It means because the kingdom, power, and glory belong to God, we can claim the provisions, promises, and protection of this prayer. When we arrive at this final portion of the model prayer and declare "Yours is the kingdom," we are coming into agreement with everything God says about His kingdom: "Do not fear, little flock, for it is your Father's good pleasure to give you the kingdom" (Luke 12:32). It is His kingdom, but as heirs, it is our kingdom also. It is a legacy conferred by our Father, and it pleases Him to give it to us.

The Greek word for "power" is *dunamis,* from which the English words *dynamic* and *dynamite* come. When we end our prayer with "Yours is the power," we are acknowledging the dynamic power of God with its dynamite-like potential for fulfilling our petitions. When we declare "Yours is the power," God echoes back to us the words of Jesus: "I give you power over all the power of the enemy." This assures the answer to all we have interceded for in the model prayer. We then declare, "Yours is the glory!" Glory is one of the richest words of the English language. No single word can serve as a good synonym, but here are some words that describe it: honor, praise, splendor, radiance, power, exaltation, worthiness, likeness, beauty, renown, and rank.

Jesus said, "And the glory which you gave Me, I have given them that they may be one just as We are one" (John 17:22). The same glory with which Jesus was glorified by the Father is a gift to us. All we have to do is claim it. You should be going from glory to glory, not from defeat to defeat. You may be discouraged, despondent, and feel cold and lifeless spiritually, but the Word of the Lord to you today is this: "Arise, shine; for your light has come! And the glory of the Lord is risen upon you." (Isaiah 60:1-2).

God's glory guarantees the following:

- Provision – "And my God shall supply all your need according to His riches in glory by Christ Jesus" (Philippians 4:19). "That He would grant you, according to the riches of His glory, to be strengthened with might through His Spirit in the inner man" (Ephesians 3:16).
- Strength – "Strengthened with all might, according to His glorious power, for all patience and longsuffering with joy" (Colossians 1:11).
- Joy – Hear the word of the Lord, You who tremble at His word: "Your brethren who hated you, who cast you out for My name's sake, said, 'Let the Lord be glorified, that we may see your joy.' But they shall be ashamed" (Isaiah 66:5). "Whom having not seen you love. Though now you do not see Him, yet believing, you rejoice with joy inexpressible and full of glory" (1 Peter 1:8). "Glory in His holy name; let the hearts of those rejoice who seek the Lord!" (1 Chronicles 16:10).
- Liberty – "Arise, shine; for your light has come! And the glory of the Lord is risen upon you" (Isaiah 60:1).
- Rest – "And in that day there shall be a Root of Jesse, who shall stand as a banner to the people; for the Gentiles shall seek Him, and His resting place shall be glorious" (Isaiah 11:10).
- Sanctification – "And there I will meet with the children of Israel, and the tabernacle shall be sanctified by My glory" (Exodus 29:43).
- Unity with other believers – "And the glory which You gave Me I have given them, that they may be one just as We are one" (John 17:22).

The word *forever* means that which is "eternal, or has no end." As we conclude our prayer, we are ascribing the kingdom, power, and glory to our Father—*forever*. We are linking ourselves in an eternal bond with our Father because we are acknowledging that we share in His kingdom, power, and glory.

## The Armor of God!

"Put on the whole armor of God, that you may be able to stand against the wiles of the devil" (Ephesians 6:11).

Are you ready to get into militant warfare prayers? It is important to put on the whole armor of God so that you can stand against the works of evil.

> Finally, my brethren, be strong in the Lord and in the power of His might. Put on the whole armor of God that you may be able to stand against the wiles of the devil. For we do not wrestle against flesh and blood, but against principalities, against powers, against the rulers of the darkness of this age, against spiritual *hosts* of wickedness in the heavenly *places.* Therefore take up the whole armor of God that you may be able to withstand in the evil day, and having done all, to stand. Stand therefore, having girded your waist with truth, having put on the breastplate of righteousness, and having shod your feet with the preparation of the gospel of peace; above all, taking the shield of faith with which you will be able to quench all the fiery darts of the wicked one. And take the helmet of salvation, and the sword of the Spirit, which is the word of God; praying always with all prayer and supplication in the Spirit, being watchful to this end with all perseverance and supplication for all the saints (Ephesians 6:10-18).

**Belt of Truth:** "I place around my waist the belt of truth. I will know the truth and the truth will make me free. I am free because whoever the Son sets free is free indeed. I am free from (say whatever you have been set free from). I am a son (or daughter) of God. The Holy Spirit guides me into all truth. He will guide me with His eye. I have the wisdom and knowledge of God. The Holy Spirit will instruct me in the way I should go."

**Breastplate of Righteousness:** "I put on the breastplate of righteousness. Because of the cross, Jesus has placed on me a robe of righteousness. I am the righteousness of God. I plead the blood of

Jesus over myself today. Forgive me of my sins this day. Convict me, Holy Spirit, of any wrong, and search my heart of any secret sin. The righteous are as bold as a lion. I thank You for boldness to do Your will today. Help me to speak Your Word with great boldness. I am established today in Your righteousness."

**The Gospel of Peace:** "My feet are shod with the preparation of the gospel of peace. Help me to be prepared to give my testimony today. I thank You that You have made a covenant with me, that Your laws and Your words are written on my heart and in my mind. You said that You put Your words in my mouth. Let my life reflect the gospel of peace. Send someone across my path with whom I can share the gospel today. Use me, Lord, to bless someone today."

**Shield of Faith:** "I take up the shield of faith that quenches every fiery dart of the enemy. Faith is the victory that overcomes the world. I am an overcomer in you. I can do all things through Christ who strengthens me. I thank You for my angels. I have an angel of the Lord who encamps around me. I am protected from the evil one and delivered from the evils of this present world."

**Helmet of Salvation:** "I place on my head the helmet of salvation, the hope of glory. I have the mind of Christ, and no weapon formed against my mind will prosper. I think of things that are good, pure, perfect, and lovely. I will take authority over my mind today. I have authority over all the power of the enemy. I choose to cast down every vain imagination that exalts itself against the knowledge of God, and I will bring them into captivity to the obedience of Christ. I belong to Jesus, and I give the Holy Spirit control of my thoughts. I submit my mind to God. I resist the devil, and he must flee."

**Sword of the Spirit:** "I take the sword of the Spirit, and I use it on the offense. I will not shrink back. I am a soldier for Christ. I wrestle against principalities. I thank You for the power of Your Word. It is sharper than any two-edged sword. It will not return void, but it accomplishes the task it was sent for. Your Word is true. You are not a man that You would lie. I am a doer of Your Word. Your Word is a lamp unto my feet and a light unto my path. I will hide Your Word in my heart so that I will not sin against you."

## Putting on the Armor of God
### Militant Prayer of Preparation

"I am strong in You, Lord, empowered through my union with you. I draw strength from you, that strength which Your boundless might provides. I put on the whole armor, which you supply, God, that I may be able to successfully stand up against all the strategies and deceits of the devil. For I wrestle not with flesh and blood, but against the principalities, against the powers, against the master spirits who are the world rulers of this present darkness, against the spirit forces of wickedness in the heavenly sphere.

"Therefore, I put on your complete armor, God that I may be able to resist and stand my ground. I stand, and I hold my ground, having tightened the girdle of truth around my loins, having put on the breastplate of righteousness (integrity, moral rectitude, right standing with God), and having shod my feet in preparation, promptness, and readiness with the gospel of peace. I lift up over all the covering shield of faith, with which I can quench all the flaming missiles of the wicked one. I take the helmet of salvation and the sword of the Spirit, which is the Word of God.

"I pray at all times, on every occasion, in every season, in the Spirit, with all manner of prayer and entreaty. I keep alert and watch with strong purpose and perseverance, interceding on behalf of all the saints. I pray that freedom of utterance may be given me, that I may speak boldly the mystery of the gospel for which I am an ambassador. I pray I may declare it boldly and courageously as I ought to do, *going to work* in Jesus' name, Amen!"

# Chapter Seven:
# Your Spiritual Authority

> And Jesus came and spoke to them, saying, "All authority has been given to Me in heaven and on earth. [19] Go therefore and make disciples of all the nations, baptizing them in the name of the Father and of the Son and of the Holy Spirit."
> Matthew 28:18-19

What God has to say about *authority* probably is a lot different than what we would like to think He has to say. Often we could consider that when we have the Holy Spirit in us, we can do anything, including ignoring the possibility of evil spirits having any effect on us. On the other hand, we could ignore the fact that when the Holy Spirit entered us at Salvation, Jesus Christ gave us the authority to stand for Him. Both these stances are so dangerous, both to our families and to us, causing us all to fail to realize our potential in Him, or to reach the fullness of His life for us. In the scriptures, our God teaches us that we both have the authority and we are to use it. Consider the teaching in Ephesians chapter 6 verses 10-18.

Understanding your spiritual authority is very important when casting out demons, healing the sick, and exercising your authority over the powers of darkness. You have been given authority to cast out demons, but instead you are praying that God brings the demon out. When you do that, you are basically asking God to do something that He gave you the tools to do yourself. Jesus told you to cast out demons. Nowhere in the Bible does it tell us to ask God to cast out demons.

You must understand that authority doesn't beg, authority doesn't ask—authority commands. You are not told to ask God to cast out demons, or to beg demons to come out. You are told to CAST them out. In Matthew 8:8-9; 13, "The centurion answered and said, 'Lord, I am not worthy that You should come under my roof. But only speak a word, and my servant will be healed. For I also am a man under authority, having soldiers under me. And I say to this one, "Go," and he goes; and to another, "Come," and he comes; and to my servant, "Do this," and he does it.' Then Jesus said to the centurion, 'Go your way, and as you have believed, *so* let it be done for you.' And his servant was healed that same hour."

Authority is exercised through your spoken word. The power of life and death are in the spoken word: "Death and life *are* in the power of the tongue, and those who love it will eat its fruit" (Proverbs 18:21). Jesus' own authority made it clear that He was the son of God, because He exercised authority that no one else had access to in history!

He cast out demons using His authority. "Then they were all amazed, so that they questioned among themselves, saying, 'What is this? What new doctrine *is* this? For with authority He commands even the unclean spirits, and they obey Him'" (Mark 1:27).

He cast out demons with His spoken word. "When evening had come, they brought to Him many who were demon-possessed. And He cast out the spirits with a word, and healed all who were sick" (Matthew 8:16).

He healed the sick with His spoken word. "Therefore, I did not even think myself worthy to come to You. But say the word, and my servant will be healed." Also, John 5:8 says, "Jesus said to him, 'Rise, take up your bed and walk.' And immediately the man was made well, took up his bed, and walked."

Jesus has been given authority over everything. "And Jesus came and spoke to them, saying, 'All authority has been given to Me in heaven and on earth'" (Matthew 28:18).

He has the authority to heal. Jesus said to "Heal the sick, cleanse the lepers, raise the dead, cast out demons. Freely you have received, freely give" (Matthew 10:8). I think it's interesting how Jesus didn't tell us to pray and ask God to heal the sick; He told us to heal the sick.

I have never seen where Jesus prayed, "Father, please heal this person!" Instead, we see that Jesus healed people with His spoken Word. In John 5:8, "Jesus said to him, 'Rise, take up your bed and walk.'"

The early church healed people in this same manner. In Acts 3:6, "Then Peter said, "Silver and gold I do not have, but what I do have I give you: In the name of Jesus Christ of Nazareth, rise up and walk."

In Luke 9:1, Jesus did not only give His disciples authority over all devils, but also to cure diseases: "Then He called His twelve disciples together and gave them power and authority over all demons, and to cure diseases." Authority is exercised when there is a RIGHT to exercise it. They were not praying and asking God to heal people; they had the authority to heal, and they were exercising it with a spoken word, just as Jesus did!

While authority plays a fundamental role in healing people, I also want you to know that prayer can do the same as it is stated in James 5:14-15. "Is anyone among you sick? Let him call for the elders of the church, and let them pray over him, anointing him with oil in the name of the Lord. [15]And the prayer of faith will save the sick, and the Lord will raise him up. And if he has committed sins, he will be forgiven." I have seen and heard of many healings that took place through prayer, so I'm not saying not to pray, or that prayer doesn't work. I'm simply saying that we have authority over sickness. Therefore, we can exercise our authority to bring about healing in another person's life.

I also think it's interesting how Mark 16:17-18 tells us that healing can come through the laying of hands. "And these signs will follow those who believe: In My name they will cast out demons; they will speak with new tongues; they will take up serpents; and if they drink anything deadly, it will by no means hurt them; they will lay hands on the sick, and they will recover." The laying of hands can encourage the transferring of power from us into the person and heal them, just like the woman who felt power flow from Jesus when she touched the hem of His garment. "And Jesus, immediately knowing in Himself that power had gone out of Him, turned around in the crowd and said,

"Who touched My clothes?" (Mark 5:30) Jesus said that those who believe will have the Holy Ghost flowing out of their innermost being. "He who believes in Me, as the Scripture has said, out of his heart will flow rivers of living water." But this He spoke concerning the Spirit, whom those believing in Him would receive, for the Holy Spirit was not yet given, because Jesus was not yet glorified" (John 7:38-39). Even Peter's shadow healed people. "So that they brought the sick out into the streets and laid them on beds and couches, that at least the shadow of Peter passing by might fall on some of them" (Acts 5:15).

Jesus distributes His authority in Mark 13:34, "It is like a man going to a far country, who left his house and gave authority to his servants, and to each his work, and commanded the doorkeeper to watch."

Jesus gives us authority through Jesus' name. The authority Jesus gives His people is not to be used in their name, but Jesus' name: "Then the seventy returned with joy, saying, 'Lord, even the demons are subject to us in Your name'" (Luke 10:17). "And these signs will follow those who believe: In My name they will cast out demons; they will speak with new tongues" (Mark 16:17). "Then Peter said, 'Silver and gold I do not have, but what I do have I give you: In the name of Jesus Christ of Nazareth, rise up and walk'" (Acts 3:6). To use somebody's authority through their name is quite an honor. It's like being able to go to the bank and draw out a million dollars on behalf of a wealthy businessman.

Jesus' authority has been given to "them who believe." Jesus gave His disciples authority to carry out His will here on earth, but they weren't the only ones. He also gave ALL believers authority to heal the sick and cast out devils when He said, "And these signs will follow those who believe: "In My name they will cast out demons; they will speak with new tongues; they will take up serpents; and if they drink anything deadly, it will by no means hurt them; they will lay hands on the sick, and they will recover" (Mark 16:17-18).

Jesus gives us authority which we can access through faith. There is a lot to be learned from the story told in Mark 9:17-29 about how faith allows us to access our authority. When the disciples came across an unusually strong demon that would not budge (verse 18), Jesus made it clear that they lacked faith by calling them faithless (verse 19). He also made it clear that some demons are so strong that a higher than usual level of faith is required to cast them out (verses 28 and 29), and that we can gain that higher level of faith through prayer and fasting (verse 29).

> "Nor do they put new wine into old wineskins, or else the wineskins break, the wine is spilled, and the wineskins are ruined. But they put new wine into new wineskins, and both are preserved." While He spoke these things to them, behold, a ruler came and worshiped Him, saying, "My daughter has just died, but come and lay Your hand on her and she will live." So Jesus arose and followed him, and so *did* His disciples. And suddenly, a woman who had a flow of blood for twelve years came from behind and touched the hem of His garment. For she said to herself, "If only I may touch His garment, I shall be made well." But Jesus turned around, and when He saw her He said, "Be of good cheer, daughter; your faith has made you well." And the woman was made well from that hour. When Jesus came into the ruler's house, and saw the flute players and the noisy crowd wailing, He said to them, "Make room, for the girl is not dead, but sleeping." And they ridiculed Him. But when the crowd was put outside, He went in and took her by the hand, and the girl arose. And the report of this went out into all that land. When Jesus departed from there, two blind men followed Him, crying out and saying, "Son of David, have mercy on us!" And when He had come into the house, the blind men came to Him. And Jesus said to them, "Do you believe that I am able to do this?"
>
> They said to Him, "Yes, Lord." Then He touched their eyes, saying, "According to your faith, let it be to you" (Matthew 9:17-29).

# Chapter Eight:
# Militant and Spiritual Warfare Prayers

"And they were helped against them, and the Hagrites were delivered into their hand, and all who *were* with them, for they cried out to God in the battle. He heeded their prayer because they put their trust in Him."

1 Chronicles 5:20

One of Satan's main objectives upon the earth today is to fight and war against you and all who are holy and righteous. From the moment you begin to live for God, Satan will challenge your walk with Him. That is why it is imperative that you stay in warfare prayer at all times and remember that your main source of power is God. Ephesians 6:18 says, "Praying always with all prayer and supplication in the Spirit, being watchful to this end with all perseverance and supplication for all the saints." Remember this warfare is not a struggle and fight against the people that Satan uses to attack and oppose you. but against Satan himself. Therefore, You must not war in the flesh, but in the Spirit because Satan is your adversary, and you must resist him in times of prayer and fasting by binding the evil spirits that are at work.

**Prayer of Forgiveness**

Are you harboring feelings of resentment against someone who has wronged you knowingly or unknowingly? You may be angry with God for situations that occurred in your life as a result of poor judgment. The negative feelings you are holding against others or God only serve to stagnate your walk with Him; therefore, it is important to ask God for forgiveness of your own sins and pray for the forgiveness of those who have hurt you.

Forgiveness is an act of will, not a feeling. If you pray for a person, you can be assured that you have forgiven that person. To help accept an individual and open yourself more to a particular person, picture him with the Lord Jesus and say to the Lord, "I love him because you love him." I forgive him because you forgive him. The Bible says, "bearing with one another, and forgiving one another, if anyone has a complaint against another; even as Christ forgave you, so you also must do" (Colossians 3:13).

Pray this prayer of forgiveness:

*Father, I ask today to forgive everyone in my life. I know that you will give me the strength to forgive, and I thank you that you love me more than I love myself and want my happiness more than I desire it for myself.*

*Father, I ask that you forgive me for the times when death, hard times, financial difficulties, or what I thought were punishments sent by you came into my family and I became bitter and resentful toward you, believing those who said, "Its God's will." Purify my heart and mind today. Lord, I forgive myself for my sins, faults, and failings, for all that is bad in me or that I think is bad.*

*I forgive myself, and I accept your forgiveness. Furthermore, I forgive myself for taking your name in vain, not worshiping you by attending church, for hurting my parents, getting drunk, for sins against purity, reading bad books, looking at bad movies, committing fornication and adultery. I also forgive myself for abortion, stealing, lying, defrauding, and hurting people's reputations. You have forgiven me today, and I forgive myself.*

*Thank you, Lord, for your grace at this moment. I forgive myself for any involvement in superstition, using Ouija boards, reading horoscopes, going to witch doctors, using fortune-telling, or wearing lucky charms.*

*I reject all superstition and choose you alone as my Lord and Savior. Fill me with Your Holy Spirit. Lord, I truly forgive my mother. I forgive her for all the times she hurt me, resented me, was angry with me and for all the times she punished me. I forgive her for the times she preferred my brothers and sisters over me. I forgive her for the times she told me I was dumb, ugly, stupid, the worst of the children, or that I cost the family a lot of money. For the times she told me I was unwanted, an accident, a mistake, or not what she expected, I forgive her.*

*Lord, I truly forgive my* father. *I forgive him for any lack of support, love, affection, or attention. I forgive him for any lack of time, for not giving me his companionship, for his drinking, for his arguing and fighting with my mother or the other children. For his severe punishments, for his desertion, for his absence from home, for him divorcing my mother, or for any running around, I do forgive him.*

*Lord, I extend forgiveness to my* sisters *and* brothers. *I forgive those who rejected me, lied about me, hated me, resented me, competed for my parents' love, hurt me, or physically harmed me. For those who were too severe on me, punished me, or made my life unpleasant in any way, I do forgive them.*

*Lord, I forgive my* spouse *for faults, failings, weaknesses, and those other acts or words that hurt or disturb me, and for lack of love, affection, consideration, support, attention, or communication. Jesus, I forgive my* children *for their lack of respect, obedience, love, attention, support, warmth, or understanding; for their bad habits, their falling away from the church, or any bad actions that disturb me, I also forgive them.*

*Lord God, I forgive my* in-laws—*my mother-in-law, father-in-law, son/daughter-in-law, and any other relatives by marriage—who treat my family with a lack of love. For all their words, thoughts, actions, or omissions that injure and cause pain, I forgive them.*

*Please help me to forgive my* relatives—*my grandmother and grandfather, aunts, uncles, and cousins—who may have interfered in our family, been possessive of my parents, caused confusion, or turned one parent against the other.*

*Jesus, help me to forgive my* co-workers *who are disagreeable or make life miserable for me. For those who push their work off on me, gossip about me, won't cooperate with me, or try to take my job, I do forgive them. My* neighbors *need to be forgiven, Lord. For all their noise, letting their property run down, not tying up their dogs that run through my yard, not taking in their trash cans, being prejudiced, and running down the neighborhood, I do forgive them. I do forgive my pastor, elders, deacons, my* congregation, *and my* church *for their lack of support, affirmation, bad sermons, pettiness, lack of friendliness, not providing me or my family with the inspiration we needed, for any hurts they have inflicted on me or my family, even in the distant past, I forgive them today.*

*Lord, I forgive all those who are of different* persuasions, *those of opposite political views who have attacked me, ridiculed me, discriminated against me, made fun of me, or economically hurt me.*

*I forgive those of different religious* denominations *and* beliefs *that have harassed me, attacked me, argued with me, and forced their views on me or my family. Those who have harmed me ethnically, discriminated against me, mocked me, made jokes about my race or nationality, hurt my family physically, emotionally, or economically, I do forgive them today.*

*Lord, I forgive all* professional people *who have hurt me in any way: doctors, nurses, lawyers, judges, politicians, and civil servants. I forgive all policemen, firemen, bus drivers, hospital workers, and especially repairmen who have taken advantage of me in their work.*

*Lord, I forgive my* employer *for not paying me enough money, for not appreciating my work, for being unkind and unreasonable with me, for being angry or unfriendly, for not promoting me, and for not complimenting me on my work.*

*Lord, I forgive both my present and past school teachers and instructors. For those who punished me, humiliated me, insulted me, treated me unjustly, made fun of me, called me dumb or stupid, or made me stay after school, I truly forgive them today.*

*Lord, I forgive my friends who have let me down, lost contact with me, did not support me, and were not available when I needed help borrowed money and did not return it, or gossiped about me. Lord Jesus, I especially pray for the grace of forgiveness for the one person in life who has hurt me the most.*

*I forgive anyone whom I consider my greatest enemy, the one who is the hardest to forgive, or the one whom I said I would never forgive. Lord, I ask for your forgiveness for the hurt I have inflicted on others, especially my mother and father, and my marriage partner. Thank You, Jesus, that I am being freed of the evil of unforgiveness. Let Your Holy Spirit fill me with light, and let every dark area of my mind be enlightened.*

## Prayer for Deliverance from Sin

Repeat this prayer below. It will bring deliverance from sin and unrighteousness, because He is able and just to forgive you. In the book of Romans 3:21-25, it is said, "But now the righteousness of God apart from the law is revealed, being witnessed by the Law and the Prophets, even the righteousness of God, through faith in Jesus Christ, to all and on all who believe. For there is no difference; for all have sinned and fall short of the glory of God, being justified freely by His grace through the redemption that is in Christ Jesus, whom God set forth as a propitiation by His blood, through faith, to demonstrate His righteousness, because in His forbearance God had passed over the sins that were previously committed."

*Lord Jesus Christ, I believe you died on the cross for my sins and rose again from the dead. You redeemed me by your blood. I belong to you, and I want to live for You. I confess all my sins, known and unknown. I renounce them all, forgive me now and cleanse me with your blood.*

*Lord, I thank you for the blood of Jesus Christ, which cleanses me now from all sin.*

*I come to you now as my deliverer. You know my special needs; the things that bind that torment and defile— that evil spirit and that unclean spirit. I claim the promise of your Word, "Whosoever that calleth on the name of the Lord shall be delivered." I call upon you now. In the name of the Lord Jesus Christ, deliver me and set me free. Satan, I renounce you and all your works. I loosen myself from you, in the name of Jesus, and I command you to leave me right now, in Jesus' name. Amen.*

**Prayer for Deliverance from Soul Ties**

The Bible says in Deuteronomy 11:26-28: "Behold, I set before you today a blessing and a curse: the blessing, if you obey the commandments of the Lord your God which I command you today; and the curse, if you do not obey the commandments of the Lord your God, but turn aside from the way which I command you today, to go after other gods which you have not known."

**Pray this prayer for deliverance from soul ties:**

*Father, I forgive my ancestors and descendants and anyone else who has sinned against me, and I ask you to forgive and bless them with all spiritual blessings. Forgive me for my sins, and I forgive myself for the sins which I committed against my body.*

*I break all curses, charms, spells, jinxes, psychic powers, hexes, vexes, and demonic ties that bind me. I break all soul ties caused by witchcraft, sorcery, bewitchment, or sexual sins. Precious Jesus, restore my fragmented soul, mind, will, and emotions. Send your angels to recover anything that was stolen from me.*

*Father, stir up the demons in my subconscious mind so that they can be identified and cast out. All these things I ask in the blessed name of* my Lord, Master and Savior Jesus Christ. I now take authority over Satan and all the forces of evil according to the whole Word of God and command that they obey it. In the name of Jesus Christ, I ask these things. Amen!

## Prayer for Deliverance from Demonic Spirits

Foul and evil spirits can torment people easily. The Bible says, "Behold, I give you the authority to trample on serpents and scorpions, and over all the power of the enemy, and nothing shall by any means hurt you" (Luke 10:19). If you are facing any form of torment from these spirits, pray this prayer for deliverance from their demonic powers:

*In the authority of Jesus Christ, I take authority over all foul and evil spirits, authorities, princes, kings, powers, world rulers, and the highest and mightiest servants of Satan.*

*I bind them to be powerless in the mighty name of Jesus Christ. Father, in the authority of the Lord Jesus Christ, I pronounce the judgment written in the scriptures upon the evil and greedy conspirators in and over these worldwide organizations.*

*As it is written, Father, I ask you to bring upon them the judgments found in Jeremiah 17:5–6, which says, "Cursed is the man who trusts in man and makes flesh his strength, whose heart departs from the Lord. For he shall be like a shrub in the desert, and shall not see when good comes, but shall inhabit the parched places in the wilderness, in a salt land which is not inhabited."*

## Prayer for Healing from Sickness

*God promised us healing because His Word says healing is the children's bread. The Bible says in Isaiah 53:5: "But He was wounded for our transgressions, He was bruised for our iniquities; the chastisement for our peace was upon Him. And by his stripes we are healed." Pray this prayer for your healing:*

*Father, I stand on the promises of your word and I bind the spirit of infirmity. I command you spirit of infirmity and all your underlings to leave my body now, in the name of Jesus Christ. I break every curse of sickness, infirmity, and organ failure. I command my body to respond to the blessing of healing and health.*

*My body is the temple of the Holy Spirit. I desire a clean temple for the Holy Spirit to dwell. Father, I confess to you my sins, failures, lack of faith, and weakness. Help me to trust You in the things I do not know. I command the spirit of confusion to leave now, in the name of Jesus Christ. Lord, I ask you to grant me the blessings of long life and good health in the service of the kingdom of God.*

*The seventy-years-plus blessings and the abundant life Jesus came to bring are your purpose for believers. I cancel the purpose and plan of the devil to kill, steal, and destroy. I refuse any part of his plan and send all his curses back to the sender now, in the name of the Lord Jesus Christ.*

*In the name of Jesus Christ, I command the body-detoxification system to be healed and every spirit that is working to be destroyed. You must leave me now. All doubt and unbelief must leave. I rebuke you now, in the name of Jesus Christ.*

*I loosen the ministering spirits for the heirs of salvation to come and minister to me now, in Jesus' name. Thank You, Lord Jesus, for providing me with victory over hell, death, and the grave, and the power over the spirits of sickness and all the power of the devil.*

*I ask to live so that I can accomplish all that God has purposed for my life. Let me be a positive influence for Christ each day. I break the curses of sickness, infirmity, organ failure, godlessness, nests of demons, doorways for demons, idolatry of possessions, and ungodly holidays.*

*I break the curses listed in the book of Deuteronomy, chapters 27 and 28, and in the rest of the Bible; from the diseases of Egypt; from every sickness and plague in the book of law that I have the legal right to break.*

*Lord, I ask that you show me any legal rights that Satan has in my life so that I may repent and break those curses. In the name of Jesus Christ, I pray. Amen!*

**Prayer for Divine and Perfect Health**

*Praying daily is very important. Ask God for His blessings and strength for the day, and command the day to be blessed and be divine according to His will. The Bible says in 3 John 1:2, "Beloved, I pray that you may prosper in all things and be in health, just as your soul prospers." Pray this prayer for divine and perfect health:*

*Dear heavenly and gracious Father, thank You for divine health—mental, physical, spiritual, and material—for me and my family. Thank You for all blessings known and unknown, and for showering down blessings on me and my family, so great, that we cannot receive them.*

*Thank You for the complete restoration of our bodies. Thank You for restoring everything that the devil has stolen from me and my entire family. Lord, let my day be blessed in everything that I do as it is written that everything I put my hands on shall be made prosperous. Bless my going out and my coming in. Let your angels of protection cover me throughout the day, in Jesus' name, amen.*

**Prayer against Financial Crisis**

Having unicorns, statues of Buddha, elephants, or frogs, a statue of a tiger representing Durga (an Indian god), Chinese bamboo plants, or an Italian horn in your home can lead to financial problems. Pray this prayer against financial crisis:

*Father, in Jesus' name, I bind all demons that would cause me to have job failure or financial failure. I bind all demons that would keep me from receiving all money, possessions, inheritance, jobs, promotions, bonuses, or raises that are rightfully mine. In Jesus' name, I command the demons to return these to me sevenfold. Father, I ask that You send your angels out to gather these and bring them to me, in Jesus' name. I release the blessings of Deuteronomy 28 upon me, in Jesus' name. Amen!*

**Prayer for Financial Breakthrough**

Are your finances under attack? Are you living paycheck to paycheck? Pray this prayer for financial breakthrough:

*Dear Jesus, I repent of any sin or disobedience of my ancestors that has allowed financial curse or hardship to prevail against me. I destroy every satanic altar and covenant that is directly responsible for financial hardship and difficulties in my life.*

*I destroy the spirit of poverty that was inherited through the bloodline, and I bind all family curses of poverty. I break every satanic chain of poverty. I renounce and reverse every financial curse, through the blood of the eternal covenant.*

*I bind and destroy the activities of anti-harvest forces. I destroy all spiritual padlocks that lock out wealth from coming into my life, in Jesus' name. I destroy every device of the enemy to divert my wealth through sickness, sudden death, accidents, and financial emergencies.*

*I erase, through the blood of Jesus Christ, every mark or handwriting of poverty on my life. I command every leaking pocket, purse, and wallet to be sealed in Jesus' name. I command the builders of financial roadblocks in my life to be arrested. I issue a warrant, pursue arrest, destroy, and terminate their assignments.*

*I pull down every financial roadblock and command the crooked places to be made straight, valleys to be exalted, and mountains to be brought low so that my financial miracles can arrive to me with speed. I command my financial deserts and wildernesses to be turned into springs and pools of living water.*

*I bind every spirit of unfruitfulness. I command my barren ground to be healed, and I declare that my labor shall not be in vain. I destroy the operations of the spirit of indebtedness over my life, in Jesus' name.*

*With the fire of God, I destroy every garment of poverty that the enemy has put on me. I command new garments of favor, wealth, and prominence to be divinely put on me. I pray, dear Lord, that you would anoint my eyes to see Your opportunities and provision.*

*I now renew my commitment to You, dear God, in the area of tithes, offerings, and vows. I command every closed heaven to be opened and to release an outpouring of the blessings of God upon my life. Free the channels of my financial blessings, dear Lord.*

*I release the anointing for wealth and prosperity to flow mightily upon my life. I declare that from now on I will enter into my season of financial conquest and triumph. I command into manifestation my seasons of divine opportunity, money, and blessing to be restored with interest. I demand wholeness in every dimension in my life, in Jesus' name. Amen!*

## Prayer for Spiritual House Cleaning

Remove all ungodly objects from your house before praying. This prayer will bring cleanliness, physically and spiritually, in your house. Use a bottle of anointing oil or let a minister of the Gospel pray over a bottle of water and sprinkle it all over the house while praying this prayer. The anointing oil will anoint the house or the water can be used as a point of contact to wash unclean things spiritually. The Bible says in Matthew 12:44: "Then he says, 'I will return to my house from which I came. And when he comes, he finds it empty, swept, and put in order.'" Pray this prayer during your spiritual house cleaning:

*Father, in your name, I command all demons by these names or associated with these objects to go:*

- *Books and objects identified with anything related to Satan's kingdom.*
- *Pictures and images and incenses that demonstrate Hinduism, Islam, or Buddhism.*
- *Sinful activities of former residents who left curses; I break those curses.*
- *Knocking or noisy ghosts (poltergeist) and apparitions.*
- *Owl and frog images of all types.*
- *Witch masks and fetishes used by witch doctors.*
- *Objects and literature that pertain to false religions or cults, the occult, and Spiritism.*
- *Graven images of gods.*
- *Objects dedicated to demons (idols and artifacts).*
- *Ouija boards or other occult paraphernalia.*
- *Prayers and worship to demons that bring curses on homes; I break those curses.*
- *Mexican sun gods; idols and incense; Buddha's; hand-carved objects from Africa or the Orient; anything connected with astrology, horoscopes, fortune-telling, good-luck charms; cult religions, metaphysics, Christian Science, and rock-and-roll records and tapes.*
- *Jewelry given to me by someone that has witchcraft, hex signs, or ancient geometric and mystical motifs; jewelry designed to bring good luck and act as a talisman to chase evil.*
- *Indian ankh, broken-cross peace symbol, Polynesian tikes, African jujus, Italian horn, protectors from the evil eye, hand with index and little fingers pointing upward, clovers, stars, wishbones, lucky coins, mystic medals, horseshoes, religious fetishes and statues.*
- *Products with cryptic cursed hidden secrets, occult curses.*
- *Dolls used for witchcraft and magic, puppets, cult objects, or representations of them.*

*I bind them all and set my house free in the powerful name of Jesus Christ, my deliverer. Father, your word declares in John 8:36: "Therefore, if the Son makes you free, you shall be free indeed." I declare and decree that I am free in Jesus' name. Amen!*

**Prayer for Children**

It is very important that you pray for your children on a daily basis. When the enemy is unable to enter your territory, your children usually end up being the bait that is used to draw you into his warzone. Pray this prayer for your children:

*I thank You, Lord, for the provision of this child. I thank You, Lord, for this child shall be great before You and shall do exploits in Your name. I decree that no sickness or plague will come upon my child, in the name of Jesus. I decree soundness, health, and wholeness into the spirit, soul, and body of my child, in the name of Jesus. I ban this child from inheriting any evil thing from our own family line, in the name of Jesus. I speak wholeness, soundness, and perfection into the heart, eyes, ears, skin, bones, teeth of my child, in the name of Jesus.*

*Let my child be covered with the blood of Jesus and surrounded by the hedge of divine fire. I disallow my child from accepting any form of infirmity, in the name of Jesus. Let the respiratory, digestive, and circulatory systems of my child be normal, strong and healthy, in the name of Jesus. O Lord, let my child be saved at an early age. O Lord, let my child be filled with the Holy Spirit even from the womb.*

*I cut off the flow of hereditary problems in my child, in the name of Jesus. I bind every negative ancestral spirit and command it to loosen its hold upon my child's life, in the name of Jesus. Let every problem arising from the power of bad parental example receive solution, in the name of Jesus. I break every hereditary curse and bondage upon my child, in the name of Jesus. Let my child be cleansed from every hereditary problem, in the blood of Jesus. I command everything that will prevent my child from being a blessing to be totally shattered, in the name of Jesus. I command any power that wants to convert my child to a nuisance to be completely paralyzed, in the name of Jesus.*

*You spirit of (pick from the under-listed), release my child, in the name of Jesus.*

- Rejection — *abnormal fears* — *familiar spirit*
- Sexual lust — *addiction* — *unreasonable silence*
- Rebellion — *forgetfulness* — *anger*
- Mind darkness — *confusion* — *day dreaming*
- Stupidity — *slowness* — *inactivity*
- Inability to read — *infirmity* — *indifference*
- Dullness — *spiritual blindness* — *ostrich behavior*
- Bad sleeping — *bad dreams*

*Let every problem arising from (pick from the under-listed); receive divine solution, in the name of Jesus.*

- *Child birth after long and protracted labor*
- *Child birth by caesarean operation or with instrumental assistance*
- *Child birth with cord around neck*
- *Father dying or leaving the mother*
- *Polygamous setup*
- *Parental addiction to alcohol, smoking or other sins*
- *Child conceived outside wedlock*
- *Child conceived as a result of rape or accidental pregnancy*
- *Child conceived as a result of incest*
- *Child born to parents who did not want them*
- *Child being spoilt or pampered*
- *Child born to unhappy parents who argue, fights, or do not communicate*
- *Child born to harsh parents*

- *Destruction of home by fire or encountering some natural disasters*
- *Sudden drop in family standard of living*
- *Child not being believed when telling the truth*
- *Constant criticism by parents*
- *Unjust discipline*
- *Subjection to sexual molestation*
- *Children with some birth deformity*
- *Children born with sex opposite to what the parents desired*
- *Sexual aggression to wife by a father in the presence of the child*
- *Adopted child*
- *Separation or divorce of the parents*
- *Death of one or both parents*
- *Boarding school*
- *Lack of parental love or discipline*
- *Attempted abortion during pregnancy, etc.*

*I render every bad spirit powerless in the life of (put the name of the child), in Jesus' name.*

*I bind the power of and break the influence of every negative spirit militating against (put the name of the child), in Jesus' name.*

*You harmful hereditary and other wicked spirits, loosen (put the name of the child) in the name of Jesus.*

*Father Lord, let the blood of Jesus cleanse the mind, emotions, imaginations and will of (put the name of the child), in the name of Jesus.*

*Lord, fill this child with Your glory, peace, and love. Thank you God for answering my prayer.*

## Prayer to Release Godly Spirits

As you pray this prayer, it will release Godly spirits into your life and around your house. It is very important to know that only the Spirit of God can help you. The Bible says in 2 Corinthians 3:17: "Now the Lord is the Spirit; and where the Spirit of the Lord is, there is liberty." Pray this prayer to release Godly spirits into your life:

*Lord Jesus Christ, I ask that you direct the angels to minister to my needs. I loosen warring angels, ministering angels, the Holy Spirit, and the sevenfold Spirit of God. I loosen hosts of angels, including the following Godly spirits, into my house and my life:*

*Spirit of wisdom, spirit of the true and living God, Holy Spirit, free spirit, faithful spirit, good spirit, humble spirit, excellent spirit, spirit of Elijah, spirit of holiness, quickening spirit, patient spirit, spirit of judgment, spirit of knowledge, new spirit, poor in spirit, spirit of your Father, strong in spirit, spirit of truth, spirit of adoption, spirit of meekness, and all the fruits of the Spirit. I now activate the fruits of the spirit according Galatians 5:22-23: "But the Fruits of the Spirit is love, joy, peace, longsuffering, kindness, goodness, faithfulness, gentleness, self-control. Against such there is not law." I now release the fruit of the Spirit in my house, my life, and my family in Jesus name, amen!*

## Prayer to Be Made Whole from Brokenness

**In Mark 5; 34, Jesus, said to the woman with the issue of blood, "Daughter,** your faith has made you well. Go in peace, and be healed of your affliction.'" Pray this prayer with all pursuit and just believe that God will make you whole just as He did to this woman:

*Heavenly Father, I bow in worship and praise before you. I cover myself with the blood of the Lord Jesus Christ as my protection. I surrender myself to you, completely and unreservedly, in every area of my life.*

*I take a stand against all the workings of Satan that hinder my prayer life. I address myself only to the true and living God and refuse any involvement of Satan in my prayer. Satan, I command you, in the name of the Lord Jesus Christ, to leave my presence, with all your demons.*

*I bring the blood of the Lord Jesus Christ between us, you wicked devil. The blood of Jesus surrounds me like a mighty wall that you cannot penetrate. Heavenly Father, I worship you and give you praise. I recognize that you are worthy to receive all glory, honor, and praise. I renew my allegiance to you and pray that the blessed Holy Spirit would enable me in this time of prayer.*

*I am thankful, heavenly Father, that you have loved me from all eternity and that you sent the Lord Jesus Christ into the world to die as my substitute. I am thankful that the Lord Jesus Christ came as my representative and that through Him you have completely forgiven me. You have adopted me into your family; you have assumed all responsibility for me; you have given me eternal life; you have given me the perfect righteousness of the Lord Jesus Christ so that I am now justified.*

*I am thankful that in Him, you have made me complete and that you have offered yourself to me to be my daily help and strength. Heavenly Father, open my eyes that I might see how great you are and how complete your provision is for this day. I am thankful that the victory the Lord Jesus Christ won for me on the cross and in His resurrection has been given to me, and that I am seated with the Lord Jesus Christ in the heavenlies.*

*I take my place with Him in the heavenlies and recognize by faith that all wicked spirits and Satan himself are under my feet. I declare, therefore, that Satan and his wicked spirits are subject to me in the name of the Lord Jesus Christ.*

*I am thankful for the armor you have provided. I put on the girdle of truth, the breastplate of righteousness, the sandals of peace, and the helmet of salvation. I lift up the shield of faith against all the fiery darts of the enemy, and I take in my hand the sword of the Spirit- the Word of God. I choose to use your Word against all the forces of evil in my life.*

*I put on this armor and live and pray in complete dependence upon you, blessed Holy Spirit. I am grateful, heavenly Father that the Lord Jesus Christ spoiled all principalities and powers and made a show of them openly and triumphed over them in Himself. I claim all that victory for my life today.*

*I reject all the insinuations, accusations, and temptations of Satan. I affirm that the Word of God is true, and I choose to live today in the light of God's Word. I, heavenly Father, choose to live in obedience to you and in fellowship with you.*

*Open my eyes and show me the areas of my life that do not please you. Work in me to cleanse me from all ground that would give Satan a foothold against me. I do in every way stand in all that it means to be your adopted child, and I welcome all the ministry of the Holy Spirit.*

*By faith and dependence upon you, I put off the fleshly works of the evil one and stand in all the victory of the crucifixion where the Lord Jesus Christ provided cleansing from the old nature. I put on your holiness and stand in all the victory of the resurrection and the provision He has made for me to live above sin. Therefore, today I put off all forms of selfishness and put on the new nature with its love.*

*I put off all forms of fear and put on the new nature with its courage. I put off all forms of weakness and put on the new nature with its strength. I put off all forms of lust and put on the new nature with its righteousness, purity, and honesty. I trust you to show me how to make this practical in my daily life. In every way, I stand in the victory of the ascension and glorification of the Lord Jesus Christ, whereby all the principalities and powers were made subject to Him.*

*I claim my place in Christ as victorious with Him over all the enemies of my soul. Blessed Holy Spirit, I pray that you would fill me. Come into my life; break down every idol and cast out every foe.*

*I am thankful, heavenly Father, for the expression of your will for my daily life as you have shown me in your Word. I, therefore, claim all the will of God for today. I am thankful that you have blessed me with all spiritual blessings in heavenly places in Christ Jesus.*

*I am thankful that you have begotten me unto a living hope by the resurrection of Jesus Christ from the dead. I am thankful that you have made a provision so that today I can live filled with the Spirit of God with love, joy, peace, long-suffering, gentleness, goodness, meekness, faithfulness, and self-control in my life.*

*I recognize that this is your will for me, and I therefore reject and resist all the endeavors of Satan and his wicked spirits to rob me of the will of God. I refuse in this day to believe my feelings, and I hold up the shield of faith against all the accusations, distortions, and insinuations that Satan would put into my mind.*

*I claim the fullness of the will of God for my life today. In the name of the Lord Jesus Christ, I completely surrender myself to you, heavenly Father, as a living sacrifice. I choose not to be conformed to this world. I choose to be transformed by the renewing of my mind, and I pray that you would show me your will and enable me to walk in all the fullness of your will today.*

*I am thankful, heavenly Father, that the weapons of our warfare are not carnal, but mighty through God to the pulling down of strongholds, to the casting down of imaginations and every high thing that exalts itself against the knowledge of God, and brings every thought into obedience to the Lord Jesus Christ.*

*Therefore, in my own life today, I tear down the strongholds of Satan and smash the plans of Satan that have been formed against me. I tear down the strongholds of Satan against my mind, and I surrender my mind to you, blessed Holy Spirit.*

*I affirm, heavenly Father, that you have not given me the spirit of fear, but of power, and of love, and of a sound mind. I break and smash the strongholds of Satan formed against my emotions today, and I give my emotions to you. I smash the strongholds of Satan formed against my will today; I give my will to you and choose to make the right decisions of faith. I smash the strongholds of Satan formed against my body today; I give my body to you, recognizing that I am your temple. I rejoice in your mercy and goodness.*

*Heavenly Father, I pray that now and throughout this day, you would strengthen and enlighten me. Show me the way Satan is hindering and tempting me and lying and distorting the truth in my life. Enable me to be the kind of person who would please you. Enable me to be aggressive in prayer and faith.*

*Enable me to be aggressive mentally, to think about and practice your Word, and to give you your rightful place in my life. Again, I cover myself with the blood of the Lord Jesus Christ and pray that your blessed Holy Spirit would bring all the work of the crucifixion, all the work of the resurrection, all the work of the glorification, and all the work of Pentecost into my life today.*

*I surrender myself to you. I refuse to be discouraged. You are the God of all hope. You have proven your power by resurrecting Jesus Christ from the dead, and I claim in every way this victory over all the satanic forces in my life. I pray in the name of the Lord Jesus Christ, with thanksgiving and praise to you alone. Amen!*

**Prayer from Evil Inheritance**

Evil inheritance pertains to things that have been passed on from generation to generation such as poverty, family demons, curses, poor health and barrenness. "But upon Mount Zion shall be deliverance, and there shall be holiness; and the house of Jacob shall possess their possessions" (Obadiah 1:17). Pray this prayer to be delivered from the cycle of evil inheritance:

*Thank you, God, for making the provision for deliverance from any form of bondage in my life. I release myself from any inherited bondage, in Jesus' name. O Lord, send your axe of fire to the foundation of my life and destroy every evil plantation. Let the blood of Jesus flush out from my system every inherited satanic deposit, in the name of Jesus. I release myself from the grip of any problem transferred into my life from the womb, in the name of Jesus. Let the blood of Jesus and the fire of the Holy Ghost cleanse every organ in my body, in the name of Jesus. I break and loosen myself from every inherited evil covenant, in the name of Jesus. I break and loosen myself from every inherited evil curse, in the name of Jesus.*

Pray aggressively against the following evil foundations. Pray as follows: You (pick one by one from the list below), loosen your hold over my life and be purged away from my foundation, in the name of Jesus.

- Evil physical design
- Envious rivalry
- Evil dedication
- Demonic incisions
- Dream pollution
- Demonic sacrifice
- Wrong exposure to sex
- Demonic initiations
- Destructive effect of polygamy
- Unscriptural manner of conception

- parental curses
- demonic blood transfusion
- demonic alteration of destiny
- demonic marriage
- evil laying on of hands
- fellowship with family idols
- exposure to evil diviners
- inherited infirmity
- fellowship with local idols
- fellowship with demonic consultants

*O Lord, let your resurrection power come upon my (be specific).*

*I bind every spirit of death operating in my (be specific), in the mighty name of Jesus. I command every dead bone in my (be specific) to come alive, in the name of Jesus.*

*You evil hand laid on my (be specific), receive the thunder and the fire of God and be roasted, in Jesus' name.*

*I command every evil monitoring gadget fashioned against my (be specific) to be destroyed, in the name of Jesus.*

*I breathe in the life of God, and I reject every spirit of death and hell, in the name of Jesus. I recover every miracle that I have lost through unbelief, in the name of Jesus.*

*Father, let your creative power operate afresh in my (be specific), in the name of Jesus.*

*Father, let the fire of the Holy Ghost enter into my bloodstream and cleanse my system, in the name of Jesus.*

*I release my (be specific) from the cage of every household wickedness, in the name of Jesus. Let every information about my (be specific) be erased from every satanic memory, in the name of Jesus.*

*I command every evil plantation in my life to come out with all your roots, in the name of Jesus!*

*[Lay your hands on your stomach and keep repeating the emphasized area.] You evil strangers in my body, come all the way out of your hiding places, in the name of Jesus. I cough out and vomit any food eaten from the table of the devil, in the name of Jesus. [Cough them out and vomit them in faith. Prime the expulsion.]*

*Let all negative materials circulating in my bloodstream be evacuated, in the name of Jesus. I drink the blood of Jesus. [Physically swallow and drink it in faith. Keep doing this for some time.] [Lay one hand on your head and the other on your stomach or navel and begin to pray.] Holy Ghost fire, burn from the top of my head to the soles of my feet. [Begin to mention every organ of your body: your kidney, liver, intestine, blood, etc. You must not rush at this level, because the fire will actually come and you may start feeling the heat.] I cut myself off from every spirit of (mention the name of your place of birth), in the name of Jesus.*

*I cut myself off from every tribal spirit and curse, in Jesus' name. I cut myself off from every territorial spirit and curse, in the name of Jesus. Holy Ghost fire, purge my life, in the name of Jesus. I claim my complete deliverance, in the name of Jesus, from the spirit of (mention the things you do not desire in your life).*

*I break the hold of any evil power over my life, in Jesus' name.*

*I move from bondage into liberty, in the name of Jesus. I release myself from every inherited disease, in Jesus' name. Let the blood of Jesus correct any inherited defect in my body, in the name of Jesus. Let every abnormality inside my body receive divine correction, in the name of Jesus. Lord Jesus, I thank you for my deliverance.*

**Prayer for the Release of Prosperity**

*Father, I thank you for your provision in life, and I stand firm upon the promises of your Word according to Psalm 34:10: "The young lions do lack and suffer hungry, but those who seek the Lord shall not lack any good thing. I hereby declare and decree that all the security-men in charge of satanic banks that are harboring my blessing be paralyzed, in the name of Jesus. I terminate the appointment of all satanic bankers and managers, in the name of Jesus.*

*I command the thunder of God to break to pieces all the satanic strongholds harboring my properties, in Jesus' name. I possess all my properties, in the name of Jesus. Let all satanic instruments—the legal tenders and the checks*—*used against me be completely destroyed, in Jesus' name. I command all satanic clearinghouses and agents to be roasted, in the name of Jesus. I paralyze completely all satanic transactions and contracts against my life, in the name of Jesus. Let all satanic networks and computers fashioned against me be disorganized, in the name of Jesus.*

*Heavenly Father, let all the blood that has been stored up in satanic banks come forth, in the name of Jesus. I refuse to be an object for satanic transaction, in Jesus' name, or to do profitless work, in the name of Jesus. Every evil force against my handiwork be paralyzed, in Jesus' name. I send back to the sender every arrow of spiritual deposit and advance payment against my handiwork, in the name of Jesus. You my handiwork, receive divine profit, in the name of Jesus. I cover my handiwork with the fire of God, with hot coals of fire untouchable by evil forces, in the name of Jesus.*

*O Lord, put to shame every evil force that is against my handiwork. My handiwork, receive the touch of the Lord, in Jesus' name. Every tree of profitless hard work, be uprooted; profitless hard work, pack your load and go out of my life, in the name of Jesus. I will not carry any evil load forward in my life, in Jesus' name. O Lord, drain out satanic deposits from my business and handiwork. Let all strange hands and legs walk out of my business and handiwork, and let the spirit of favor fall upon me now, in the name of Jesus.*

*O Lord, enlarge my coast. I rebuke every devourer in my handiwork, in the name of Jesus. O Lord, cause ministering angels to bring in customers and money into my business. I bind every spirit of error, in the name of Jesus. Let every trouble emanating from envious business partners be rendered null and void, in the name of Jesus. O Lord, surprise me with abundance in every area of my life. I command a quit-notice to evil legs of finance, evil powers keeping the copy of my registration certificates and every operational curse, in Jesus' name.*

*Let the anointing for money-yielding ideas fall upon my life, in the name of Jesus. I bind every spirit of fake and useless investment, and I command every effect of strange money on my business to be neutralized, in the name of Jesus. Father Lord, let all satanic hosts against my prosperity receive blindness and commotion, in the name of Jesus. All hindrances to my prosperity be electrocuted, in Jesus' name. Let all my mistakes be converted to miracles and testimonies, in the name of Jesus.*

*I command all those who vow to hinder my prosperity to somersault, become naked and confess to death, in Jesus' name. I command all my buried blessings to be exhumed, in Jesus' name. Father Lord, use both white and black men to bless me, in the name of Jesus. I command all my pounds sterling and dollars' miracles to locate me, in the name of Jesus. All my blessings attached to my place of birth, be released, in the name of Jesus.*

*Father Lord, use all the people in my environment to bless me and let the anointing of prosperity fall on me, in the name of Jesus. Lord, by the power of the blood, remove from my life any hindrance of the enemy. O Lord, drive away all darkness in every area of my life, shield me from all forms of deception, and illuminate your truth to my understanding. Lord, let me, with the eyes of my heart, see you clearly. Lord, take away from me; all powers that do not originate from you. I separate myself from Satan and his kingdom, in Jesus' name.*

*I renounce the kingdom of darkness and embrace the kingdom of Jesus Christ, in the name of Jesus. Lord Jesus, deliver me from evil. I apply the blood of Jesus Christ to break all evil curses. I shall be anointed with fresh oil from heaven, in Jesus' name. Lord, reveal strongholds that hinder and give Satan advantage over me. Lord Jesus, let a deep work begin in my heart. I kill all strange animals sent against me with the sword of the Lord, in the name of Jesus. I divorce every satanic husband; let the fire of God be released on every demonic child in my family, in the name of Jesus. Let all evil spiritual homes be burnt down, in the name of Jesus.*

*I reject the spirit of slavery and hardship in every area of my life, in the name of Jesus. Let the spirit of delay and hindrance be cast out of my life, in the name of Jesus. I dissolve every anti-breakthrough strategy of the enemy, in Jesus' name. Let the hands of evil refuse to perform their enterprise in any area of my life, in the name of Jesus. I decree that there shall not be compromise and dialogue between me and my enemies, in the name of Jesus. I pull down all strongholds of evil over my life and the lives of members of my family, in the name of Jesus. Lord, close the gap between where I am and where you want me to be. Let all demonic jailers be roasted, in the name of Jesus.*

Thank the Lord for answered prayers. I now activate Philippians 4:19, which says, "And my God will meet all your needs according to the riches of his glory in Christ Jesus. Amen!"

# Declaration

"You will also declare a thing, and it will be established for you;
So light will shine on your ways."
Job 22:28

- "I decree and declare tender mercies, kindness, humility, meekness, and long-suffering over my life; and I put on love and the bond of perfection."
- "I decree and declare the peace of God to rule over my heart."
- "I decree and declare that the Word of God will dwell in my heart richly in all wisdom, teaching and admonishing others in psalms, hymns and spiritual songs, singing with grace in my heart to the Lord."
- "I decree and declare that whatever I do, I do in word and indeed in the name of Jesus, giving thanks to God the Father through Him."
- "I put on Christ because I have been baptized in Him. I put on the Lord Jesus as a garment."
- "I put on the breastplate of faith and love."
- "I put on mercy and truth around my neck."
- "I put on the armor of light."
- "I place on myself the mind of Christ. I let this mind (the mind of Christ) be in me."
- "I meditate on Your Word, day and night. You are faithful to perform Your Word. You will bring it to completion. You are faithful to complete the work You have begun in me and my life."
- "Let the meditation of my heart and the words of my mouth be pleasing unto You, O Lord. I will open my mouth, and You will fill it."
- "I place a guard on my mouth. I commit my mouth to You, Lord, that I might not sin against You."

- "You, Lord, are seated high above all authority, power, dominion, and might. Nothing is too difficult for You."
- "I place the armor of righteousness on my right and left hands."
- "I put on strength. I clothe myself with strength for the battle. You are looking for a pure heart, whose heart You can strengthen."
- "I thank You for a shield of favor around me."
- "I plead the blood over my body, mind, will, soul, and emotions. I repent of all sins. I will not fear the arrow by day or the terror by night."
- "I put on the garment of salvation. I am clothed with salvation."
- "I put on the helmet of hope."
- "I put on the robe of righteousness."
- "I put on the blue ephod."
- "I ask for the fear of the Lord, which is the beginning of wisdom."
- "I ask for the spirit of wisdom, knowledge, understanding, and revelation."
- "I am anointed, appointed, called, marked, chosen, beloved, accepted, and not rejected, in Jesus' name."
- "I put on as a helmet the hope of salvation."
- "Help me, Lord, to be sober and vigilant, watchful in the Spirit, and aware of the enemy, the devil. Wake me up, spiritually."
- "I rule and reign with Christ Jesus."
- "Lord, You cover my head; You have covered my head in the day of battle."
- "The Word is my shield and buckler."
- "I loosen myself from the bonds around my neck. I tie down my enemies in the spirit realm. I reverse the words of those who curse me, send evil against me, and send evil against the work of the Lord. I send all evil back to them seven times, in the name of Jesus."
- "May they be brought to their knees and to repentance by the Lord Jesus, that they may be saved, healed, filled, and delivered, in Jesus' mighty name. I reverse every assignment,

trap, snare, wile, and evil plan or attack against me from Satan and his angels, demons, imps, principalities, rulers of the darkness, powers, spiritual hosts of wickedness in the heavenly places, or spirits of any kind. I silence them and their words or curses."

- "I cancel all assignments against me. I make all word curses null and void."
- "I ask the Lord to send legions of angels to minister to me, protect me, battle for me, minister healing and restoration, and to surround me, in the name of Jesus."
- "I love, bless, and forgive those who persecute me and say all manner of evil against me for the sake of Your righteousness."
- "Help me, Lord, to be strong in You and in Your power, to exercise the authority over the devil that You have given me, to stand against the devil, to wrestle and do warfare, to put on my armor daily, to pray without ceasing, to intercede, and to fight the good fight of faith. Amen."

# About the Author

Robin Dinnanauth is an international evangelist and deliverance minister. He ministers the gospel of the Lord Jesus Christ and demonstrates God's saving, healing, and delivering power throughout the United States and around the world. He has been used mightily by God in the ministry of healing and deliverance. He is out on the front line, battling Satan and leading the charge against demonic forces that are destroying so many lives.

He is a highly sought-after crusader and revival speaker whom god has raised up as a prophetic voice to the world. Robin Dinnanauth is on a mission to bring the lost to the cross through the good news of the gospel and power of the blood of the Lamb. His goal is to empower people through the Word of God, that they may discover the authority that God has given to them to subdue Satan's plans.

Thousands have experienced the saving, having, and delivering message of Jesus Christ as Bishop Dinnanauth ministers hope to the sick, the afflicted, and the hurting. He is known for his dynamic and anointed prayer, healing, and deliverance ministry. He is an ordained minister, a CEO, pastor, overseer, and founder of the Emmanuel Full Gospel Assemblies of Churches, Robin Healing Ministries, and RDM Institute of Spiritual Development.

He is also the author of Faith and Foundation, Power to Prosper, Waging Spiritual Warfare, Miracles Still Happen and many other books. For these and other media resources and tools by Robin Dinnanauth, you can visit RHM website at www.robinhealingministry.com

# NOTES

# NOTES

# NOTES

www.ingramcontent.com/pod-product-compliance
Lightning Source LLC
LaVergne TN
LVHW041630070426
835507LV00008B/541